HAMLET Sports Special

Cricket

HAMLET
Sports Special

Cricket

Hamlyn
London · New York · Sydney · Toronto

The photographs on the cover and title spread are:
Front cover Bob Woolmer hammers a ball from O'Keefe past an
unhelmeted Australian close fielder on his way to a century at Lord's,
first Test, 1977
Back cover Typical elegance from David Gower in the first Test
against Pakistan, Edgbaston, 1978. Wasim Bari is the wicket keeper
Title spread Geoff Boycott drives the ball back over the bowler's head
for Yorkshire against Essex at Colchester in 1971

This book was commissioned by 'Hamlet' Cigars

'Hamlet' and 'Benson and Hedges' are registered trade marks in the
United Kingdom of J. R. Freeman & Son Limited and Benson &
Hedges Limited respectively; both companies are subsidiaries of
Gallaher Limited

Acknowledgements

The pictures in this book were obtained from the following sources:
BBC Hulton Picture Library: 52; Central Press: 15 bottom, 16, 17, 23,
35, 39, 44, 45, 46, 49, 53, 57, 61 top, 62, 64, 68, 69; Hamlyn Group
Picture Library: 7, 21 bottom, 66 top; Mansell Collection: 10, 11, 12,
13, 15 top, 24, 25 bottom, 28, 29, 30-31, 31 top, 32, 33, 34; Press
Association London: 56, 59, 67 top; Sport and General London: 27,
65, 71, 72; Syndication International London: 38, 61 bottom; Tate
Gallery London: 9
The remaining photographs were supplied by Patrick Eagar

Published 1980 by
The Hamlyn Publishing Group Limited
London · New York · Sydney · Toronto
Astronaut House, Feltham, Middlesex, England

ISBN 0 600 34646 3

Phototypeset by Photocomp Limited, Birmingham, England
Printed in Italy

Contents

Introduction
Benny Green

In one of the early novels of Mr P. G. Wodehouse there occurs a passage in which an American tycoon, henpecked into taking up residence in London, cross-examines his butler on the subject of cricket. The butler, being a paragon of his species, withholds from his employer the truth, which is that it is quite impossible for any Englishman to 'explain' cricket to any foreigner in less than twenty years, and makes a polite attempt to define a few terms and disclose the intention behind some of the more elementary movements in the choreography of the game. The tycoon listens to this exposition for a while, his eyeballs glazing over ever more as the lecture proceeds; finally his brain snaps and he blurts out the blasphemy to which all foreigners come in the end: 'Exciting? How do you make that out? I sat in the bleachers all afternoon, waiting for something to break loose. Doesn't anything ever happen at cricket?'

It is an interesting question, seeing that humanity is divided into those who wonder if anything happens at cricket and those who know that everything which could conceivably happen already has. Cricket is the best-kept secret of English social life, a mystery so inscrutable that it even has devotees who, from time to time, are not sure what they are talking about. Compared to the various committees of the MCC, the inscrutable oriental is a deafening chatterbox, and I am reminded of a beloved jazz pianist of my youth called Thomas 'Fats' Waller, who, on being asked by a well-meaning lady what Jazz was, replied, 'Lady, if you gotta ask, might as well forget it' — which is, of course what Wodehouse's butler should have really replied to his tycoon.

Views of cricket vary between the 'only a game' rejection of the deskbound, to its elevation to an art-form, and even, at one point, to a religion. The truth probably lies somewhere in the middle. I do not mean by this that cricket is halfway between a mere game on the one hand and an art-form or a religion on the other, but that it wavers engagingly between art-form and religion. The Englishman is introduced to its mysteries at an age so young as to preclude retrospective analysis of the event. Whether or not the foetus retains memories of its pre-natal tribulations is a moot point, but certainly the average Englishman cannot recall when it was he first put his finger round the handle of a bat, or first lovingly picked at the stitches of a 'hard' ball. As to that apocalyptic moment in a man's life when for the first time he shuts his eyes and swings in the hope of belting one on the half volley and actually hits it with the meat of the bat, that is an occasion almost too sacred to discuss at all.

It has been said that there are already too many books about cricket. But then on the other hand there have always been loonies in this world, and the best thing that a sensible man can do is to ignore their ravings and get on with the business of life, among whose chores is the increase in the number of books about cricket. Luckily those responsible for Hamlet cigars are sensible men, and needed no persuasion therefore to decide their new sports special should be the modest but, one hopes, worthy volume which the reader now holds in his hand.

The Beginnings of Cricket

Alan Lee

Nobody alive can confidently state where, when or indeed why cricket was first played. Its origins are even now cloaked in confusion, and perhaps it is better that way. The theories, estimates and fanciful guesses are altogether more romantic for the considerable element of doubt attached.

Of some things we can be reasonably certain. The name cricket, for instance, seems likely to have derived from the Anglo-Saxon term for a staff, 'cricce', and the game itself probably had its forerunners in two more primitive sports involving bowling and hitting a ball, or object. In Scotland, at the end of the 17th century, they played 'Cat and Dog', which was apparently all about one person throwing a block of wood towards a hole in the ground, and another – armed with a club – doing his best to keep it out. Slightly earlier, and in the north of England, a game called 'Stoolball' was popular, involving a bowler, a stool for a wicket and a 'batsman' using his hand. The relevancy of this game to cricket's heritage is, however, somewhat obscured by the notion that it was chiefly played by girls...

There is certainly something alluring about the vision of the earliest games of cricket, and if I were a real-life Dr Who with my own telephone box time-machine, I would not hesitate to transport myself back to the seventeenth century and the rough, green meadows of England where the earliest Dennis Lillees were firing down their 'shooters' and the most primitive Geoff Boycotts were coping with and complaining about the uneven bounce of the cowfield wicket. At least, it must have been like that, mustn't it?

Organised cricket grew more common in the early eighteenth century, by which time two stumps were used instead of the original idea of just one. Something I have never fully understood, however, is that they were set about two feet apart – with a bail across the top – so that the most accurate of bowlers, with a consistent 'middle-stump' line, must have had a pretty lean time!

The basic, rough-and-ready matches had up to now been the business of the peasantry, but things began to alter rapidly as the game took off. Clubs were formed around the home counties and the monied squires and gentlefolk acquired an interest which was not entirely to do with the active side of the game. As a breed, they had a passion for gambling, and cricket was the perfect outlet. Individual contests – single-wicket matches as we would call them now – were popular with the betting fraternity and the participants were apparently not slow to seize upon the significance of their role. As the late Neville Cardus once put it: 'Some of them accepted a fee to do their best, not only to win, but to lose'. With that, one image is shattered. Cricket, even in those earliest times, was not quite the game of impeccable moral code that I was brought up to believe.

Nor, it seems, was it a game without violence of the tongue or the fists. In the days before an accepted set of rules, unsavoury incidents between rival teams were commonplace, and lawsuits resulting from such argy-bargy were not unusual. Cricket was in the courtrooms long before Kerry Packer's modern-day revolution.

It was in 1744 that the Laws of Cricket appeared for the first time. Compared to more recent re-issues, they were brief and to the point. 'If ye Wicket is Bowled down, its Out' is a typical extract. In that same year, we can recall with certainty that a match was played at the Artillery Ground, in Finsbury, North London, between Kent and All-England. The scorecard has been preserved from the match, which may also be the subject of at least one of the better-known earliest cricket paintings.

No account of cricket's beginnings can progress far without reference to the

Hampshire village of Hambledon, where gathered together most of the 18th-century's most distinguished players to form a club team more famous than any other, either before or since.

Strange though it may seem, these two hundred years later, Hambledon regularly played and defeated a team representing the rest of England. Their base, for their most famous years, was Broad-halfpenny Down, and their headquarters a building which survives as The Bat and Ball Inn. It was then known as 'The Hutt' and kept by Richard Nyren, captain and groundsman of this extraordinary club.

Another Nyren, the well-chronicled early cricket writer John, claims that 'No eleven in England could compare with the Hambledon, which met on the first Tuesday in May on Broad-halfpenny'. In his 1830 book, 'The Young Cricketer's Tutor', Nyren went on to relate that the men of Hambledon were so renowned that 'the whole country would flock to see one of their trial matches'.

In his colourful narrative on the characters of the side, Nyren talks of a man called Thomas Brett, a farmer who sounds the archetype boots and braces fast bowler of early times. 'He was a well-grown, dark-looking man, remarkably strong and with

rather a short arm,' he recalls. 'Brett was, beyond all comparison, the fastest as well as straightest bowler that was ever known; he was neither a thrower nor a jerker, but a legitimate, downright bowler...'

Caustic words, perhaps, as a reference to the changing face of the game, the last defence of the underarm code before the take-over by round-arm and, subsequently, over-arm bowling. The change was not a comfortable process, giving rise to as much acrimony and as many tantrums as the more recent controversies over bouncers and beamers.

The earliest method of bowling was the underarm roll, resembling the action of the bowls player. This style had its advantages on the most primitive pitches, where the roll could hardly have had a true and consistent direction. Gradually, however, the lob became more popular, bouncing only once and aimed to deceive the batsmen with flight and, sometimes, spin.

It is difficult to imagine underarm lobs, however cunningly flighted, troubling Viv Richards, but in those days batting techniques were still at a raw stage in their development. The start of the nineteenth century saw more sophisticated batting and a consequent increase in high scores. As the bowlers began to feel dominated, a

A cricket match around 1740-45 from a painting in the Tate Gallery attributed to W. R. Coates

Top *A cricket match at Hambledon in 1777, from an old print* Above *Boys tossing a cricket bat for innings, from an oil painting*

his own club turned against him. Walker was branded a 'chucker'.

Human nature being what it is, however, the bowlers of the time were rightly determined to end the growing command of bat over ball, and a persistent revolutionary by the name of John Willes actually incited a riot by bowling in round-arm style for Kent against All-England in 1807. He must have been a hardy chap, for he carried on with his experiments despite threats of physical harm and even an official line taken in 1816, when the MCC insisted that underarm bowling was still the only acceptable form. Six years later, came one of the most sensational episodes ever seen at Lord's. Willes, playing for Kent against MCC, was apparently no-balled for another round-arm attempt. His spirit broken at last by the stonewall reluctance of the game to change (where have we heard that more recently?), Willes walked off the field, jumped on his horse and rode out of the ground and out of cricket for ever.

Willes' part was that of the human sacrifice to the bowlers' cause. More and more adopted the new style, including the legendary William Lillywhite, and another look into the annals shows that Sussex were in trouble with cricket authority even in

new style was demanded, and it arrived in the contentious form of round-arm bowling.

A Hambledon bowler by the name of Tom Walker had perhaps been the pioneer of the new fashion. But his roundarm efforts in the 1780s were anything but popular. He received the sort of reaction that Harold Larwood must have felt during the Bodyline series, 150 years later, and even those days. Long before the headline controversies of Snow, Greig, Imran and Le Roux which have made them the most controversial county of the 1970s, Sussex were the subject of a signed complaint by England cricketers that they would refuse to play against the county unless they abandoned the 'unfair' round-arm bowling style.

It took four more alterations to law by the MCC before, in 1864, restrictions were lifted and all types of round-arm and overarm bowling were sanctioned. By then it was too late for the two greatest round-arm bowlers in England, Lillywhite and Alfred Mynn, to take advantage. They had died, ten years and three years earlier respectively: Lillywhite, the slow-medium exponent with the variations and intelligence to suggest an early forerunner of Derek Underwood, Mynn perhaps the first and fastest of the genuine pace bowlers of that age, a giant of six feet and eighteen stone, loved by all but the batsmen who had to face him.

I have already mentioned Lord's as a venue, but not yet touched upon the man who made it all possible. The venue came into being through a complicated saga which began with the regular fixtures held at a ground in Islington, the property of the White Conduit Inn. Cricket had been played there from the early years of the 18th century, but the aristocracy who took part – a number of whom were responsible for the revised and more authentic issue of

Below *A match for Lord's jubilee, 1837*
Bottom *An improbable catch by a spectator, Lord's, 1893*

Laws in 1774 – sought somewhere more suitable to their social standing. The Earl of Winchelsea and Charles Lennox therefore instructed Thomas Lord, a Yorkshireman of no great status, to acquire a ground himself, promising that they would supply the money.

The first ground to be called Lord's was on the current site of Dorset Square, and in 1787 Middlesex met Essex there, and the Marylebone Cricket Club came into being. Since then, Middlesex have always played at Lord's, MCC have always occupied the ground and, until challenged by recent streamlining, have always been regarded as the prime rulers of the game of cricket.

Lord's was to be re-sited twice before coming to rest on its present site in 1814, opened officially by a match between MCC and Hertfordshire on June 22. Lord himself has, of course, been immortalised by the ground, a testimony to his shrewdness having lost all the money and property once owned by his father through being on the wrong side in the rebellion of 1745.

So with the MCC in action, Lord's housing major matches and over-arm bowling finally allowed, cricket moved towards the end of the 19th century in a state not dramatically removed from to-day.

Even equipment was being brought up to date. The bat, a curved object for much of the 18th century, resembled the implements of today – though, I am sure, without the springs which so aid the modern player – three stumps were being used after some heated complaints by one of those accurate bowlers referred to earlier, and pads and gloves were being worn far more frequently.

The top hats and buckled shoes which, at our distance, made the Hambledonians and their contemporaries rather absurd cricketing figures, were also vanishing slowly, and by the time W.G. Grace took the stage and official Test cricket opened its doors, harlequin caps, flannels and boots were in vogue. Cricket was beckoning the 20th century.

The County Championship
Maurice Golesworthy

When considering the County Championship there is a problem in deciding just where to begin. 'Begin at the beginning' said the King in Lewis Carroll, but as for the competition which has been the backbone of English cricket for so many years there has been no complete agreement about when it really began.

Nowadays *Wisden* has a list which shows the 'Champion County Since 1864'. The heading is well chosen for while the press selected a 'Champion County' in each of the earliest seasons as far back as 1864 there was certainly no County Championship competition in those early days.

Generally speaking, 1873 has become accepted by most cricket historians as the starting date for the County Championship because it was then that a rule came into force which prevented a cricketer from playing for more than one county in any season, but there was still no official championship outside of the sporting press, who compiled one on the basis of least number of matches lost.

1890 is another significant year because it was then that the county secretaries first officially acknowledged a Championship. The basis at this time was one of deducting losses from wins and ignoring drawn games, and there is a strong case for proclaiming that the first side to win the County Championship was Surrey in 1890. However, if only because there is no space here to develop an argument to the contrary, there seems no reason why we should not go along with the majority and, therefore, any cumulative figures or records mentioned here are based on commencement in 1873, when the nine first-class counties finished in this order: Gloucestershire, Nottinghamshire, Middlesex, Derbyshire, Kent, Lancashire, Yorkshire, Sussex and Surrey. As the table was then decided on the basis of least matches lost, and both Gloucestershire and Nottinghamshire were undefeated, then, of course, they were bracketed together.

Incidentally, there have been many different systems of deciding the Championship since then, from one point for a win and $1\frac{1}{2}$ points for a draw, up to as many as 15 points for a win plus many other complications which can safely be ignored in this brief survey.

Of the original members just mentioned Derbyshire were first to drop out (in 1887), but Somerset were admitted in 1891, followed by Essex, Leicestershire, Hampshire and Warwickshire in 1895 when Derbyshire were also re-admitted. The final additions were Worcestershire (1899), Northamptonshire (1905) and Glamorgan (1921). Apart from the fact that Worcestershire missed season 1919 there has been no other change.

Around the time that the popularity of county cricket first established itself throughout the country in the second half of the 19th century, the strength passed from the south to the north, where the spinners and weavers had taken up the game with real enthusiasm. Thanks to the enterprise and talent of William Clarke, cricket had long been developed along sound business-like lines in Nottinghamshire and so it was this county that first established supremacy in the County Championship.

It was due largely to the prowess of their professional bowlers that the north took over from the south, and when Nottinghamshire were at the height of their power between about 1870 and 1890 their team included such bowling stars as Alfred Shaw, who was so accurate that he bowled more overs than he conceded runs, 'Dick' Attewell, Fred Morley and William Flowers, who was the first professional to complete the cricketer's 'double' (1883). In addition to their bowling strength, however, Notts were blessed with such fine batsmen as Richard Daft, William Gunn, William Oscroft, William Barnes, William Scotton and Arthur Shrewsbury, whose

Top *Arthur Shrewsbury, Notts batsman of the 19th century*
Above *William Gunn, another fine Notts batsman, whose picture still advertises cricket bats*

opening partnership of 391 with A. O. Jones at Bristol in 1899 is still a first wicket record for the county.

Such was the strength of the men of Notts that they were pronounced Champions ten times (including four shared titles) in the first 17 years of the competition, or a total of 15 times (four shared) in 26 years if one choses to begin as far back as 1864. When they won the Championship outright four seasons in succession, 1883-86, they lost only two of their 48 county matches!

Notts, not surprisingly, failed to maintain such overall supremacy, and, indeed, after sharing the title in 1889 they have since won it on only two occasions. When today we take an overall look at the Championship's history the two counties that stand supreme are Yorkshire and Surrey. Just look at this list of title wins since 1873:

	wins	shared
Yorkshire	29	1
Surrey	17	2
Lancashire	8	4
Nottinghamshire	6	6
Kent	6	1
Middlesex	5	2
Gloucestershire	3	1
Warwickshire	3	—
Worcestershire	3	—
Glamorgan	2	—
Hampshire	2	—
Derbyshire	1	—
Leicestershire	1	—
Essex	1	—

Only Northamptonshire, Somerset and Sussex have yet to win the Championship.

Yorkshire's record is one of amazing consistency and supremacy. After winning the Championship for the first time in 1893 they finished out of the top two places only eight times in the 21 years up to the outbreak of the First World War. Between the two wars it was only seven times in 21 years that they finished below second place, and while their record since the Second World War has not been quite so brilliant, especially in many of the most recent campaigns, they have still succeeded in winning the Championship nine times and finishing runner-up on six occasions.

The man who first put Yorkshire cricket on the map and helped so much to keep it there was Lord Hawke, a disciplinarian and great lover of the game. He was captain for 28 years from 1883, President from 1898 until his death in 1938, and also had spells as President and Treasurer of the MCC. His side which won the Championship three seasons in a row, 1900-01-02, is recognised as one of the finest combinations ever to grace English cricket. They had brilliant openers in J. T. Brown and John Tunnicliffe, an all-round supreme in George Hirst, and one of the greatest slow left-arm bowlers in the game's history in Wilfred Rhodes. In 1900 Rhodes created a Yorkshire record that stands to this day by taking 240 wickets (261 in all first-class matches). What club has had a finer pair of contemporary cricketers than Hirst and Rhodes? During the 20 playing seasons from 1901 to 1924 inclusive there was only one season (1902) in which neither of these two players completed the double of 100 wickets and 1000 runs.

In winning the Championship three seasons in succession Yorkshire were beaten only twice in 80 matches, and on both occasions it was Somerset who lowered their colours. The game at Leeds in 1901 was one of the most surprising ever played. Somerset were all out for 87 on the first day but subsequently recoverd from a deficit of 238 to win by 279 runs, thanks to what is still a record score against Yorkshire, 630. Somerset's opening pair, L. C. H. Palairet and L. C. Braund, put on 222 for the first wicket. Yorkshire's 1902 defeat by Somerset was also at home (Sheffield this time), but it was a low-scoring match in which Somerset's great all-rounder, Len Braund, starred by taking 6-30 and 9-41.

Yorkshire dominated both the 1920's and the 1930s. In the earlier of these two decades they were Champions four seasons in a row thanks to the all-round ability of Roy Kilner (469 wickets and 3180 runs in those four seasons for Yorkshire), and Wilf Rhodes (337 wickets and 4264 runs), and the batsmanship of Percy Holmes and Herbert Sutcliffe (6466 and 6256 runs respectively). The chief wicket-taker was G. G. Macaulay (604 wickets in the four seasons).

In the 1930s Yorkshire failed to win the Championship only three times, when they finished third, fifth and third. Herbert Sutcliffe created a Yorkshire record by scoring 2883 runs in 1932 as well as combining with Percy Holmes in that memorable first wicket stand of 555 against

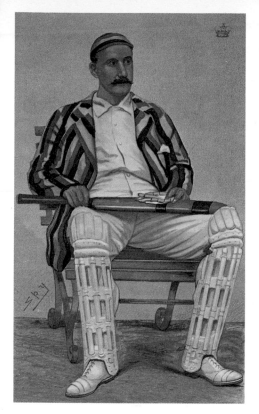

Far left *Cartoon by Spy of Lord Hawke*
Left *Another Yorkshire cricketer, another Spy cartoon: supreme all-rounder George Hirst*

Essex at Leyton. It was in the same season that Hedley Verity took 10 for 10 in an innings against Nottinghamshire at Leeds, while in the following summer this left-arm spinner took 17 Essex wickets for 91 runs at Leyton.

Probably no other county has made such consistent and successful use of local bred players than Yorkshire, and again in their latest spell at the top in the 1960s it was Yorkshiremen who put them there – Geoff Boycott, Brian Close, Ray Illingworth and Freddie Trueman, to mention only a small number.

Surrey were a power in County cricket before Yorkshire, and the southern county has since achieved something unique in this competition – winning the Championship no less than seven seasons in succession, a truly remarkable performance for any major sporting competition. However, before considering that great run of 1952-58 let us remember that Surrey were probably the first county to be widely proclaimed Champions of England (1864), or if we confine ourselves to the period in which the competition was run on more acceptable lines, then it was (with the possible exception of Nottinghamshire) Surrey that produced the first county team

of real strength in depth. Under the captaincy of John Shuter and K.J. Key they won the title eight times in nine years 1887-95, including once when they were bracketed at the top with Lancashire and Nottinghamshire.

Their top batsmen were W. W. Read (338 against Oxford University at The Oval in 1888) and little Bobby Abel (The Guv'nor) who hit 357 not out when Surrey scored 811 against Somerset at The Oval in 1899. There was no finer match-winner at this time than George Lohmann who captured 1273 wickets in seven consecutive seasons 1886-92, never dropping below 150 wickets in any of those campaigns. Towards the end of this period of Surrey supremacy they introduced another prolific wicket-taker in Tom Richardson, one of the most successful fast bowlers in the history of the Championship. In his second season (1893) he took 174 wickets, and reached his peak in 1895 with 290, a record 250 of them for Surrey. In 1894 he took all 10 Essex wickets at The Oval and his career total of 1775 wickets for Surrey has never been equalled by any other player for that county.

Richardson, however, was not the only top class fast bowler in the Surrey arma-

Hedley Verity, one of whose most impressive feats for Yorkshire was an analysis of 10 for 10 in an innings against Nottinghamshire

ment at this time, for they also had W. H. Lockwood who joined them from Nottinghamshire. This was the player who took four wickets in four balls for Surrey against Warwickshire at The Oval in 1894 (outside the Championship). Against Gloucestershire at Cheltenham in 1899 he captured 15 for 184, and performed the 'double' in 1899 and 1900.

For those casual cricket fans who believe that the scoring of runs is the be all and end all of the game, it is worth noting that during the period that Surrey were blessed with the most prolific batsman in the game's history, Jack Hobbs, they won the Championship only once (in 1914). This delightful batsman and engaging personality scored a record 43 703 runs for Surrey between 1905 and 1934, including 144 centuries. In 1907 he and Tom Hayward shared in four three-figure opening stands for Surrey in one week. At The Oval in 1919 when Surrey were left 42 minutes in which to get 95 runs to beat Kent, Hobbs and J. N. Crawford opened

their innings with 96 runs in only 32 minutes.

The record score in one day's County Championship is 645 for 4 in five hours and twenty minutes by Surrey against Hampshire at The Oval in 1909. On this occasion Hobbs was quite dazzling, scoring runs at a terrific rate and sharing in a second-wicket stand with Hayes which produced 371 in two and three-quarter hours. This is still a second wicket record for Surrey, while Hobbs' first-wicket stand of 428 with Andy Sandham against Oxford University, at The Oval in 1926, is another Surrey record. Hobbs scored a century in each innings of a County Championship match five times for Surrey. All of these runs but only one Championship from 1899 until their great post-war revival in 1950!

At this period of their history Surrey developed one of the greatest bowling and fielding sides ever to be seen in the Championship. The batting during the greater part of their seven-year run of title wins was largely in the hands of Peter May,

The County Champions of 1952, who remained champions until 1959 – the great Surrey side. Left to right, standing: Sandham (coach), Lock, Brazier, Pratt, Clark, Whittaker, E. Bedser, Laker, Loader, Kirby, McIntyre, Cox, Strudwick (scorer), Tait (masseur). Front: Fletcher, A. Bedser, Fishlock, Surridge (captain), May, Parker, Constable

Bernard Constable and Ken Barrington, but just look at this attack: A. V. Bedser, W. S. Surridge, J. C. Laker, P. J. Loader and G. A. R. Lock. For five of those seven seasons the side was under the dynamic captaincy of the burly Stuart Surridge, and he was succeeded in the other two seasons by England captain Peter May.

Some of the feats performed by this team in the 1950s are legend. Of course, Jim Laker's greatest bowling feats were achieved outside of the Championship, but he twice performed the 'hat-trick' in the Championship for Surrey. His best season in the run of seven title wins was in 1954 when he took 112 wickets (average 14·46). That was in County matches. The figure was exceeded by Tony Lock, the slow left-arm bowler who in the 1957 Championship-winning campaign took 153 wickets (average 11·58), which is one of the finest bowling averages ever recorded in this competition. Against Kent at Blackheath in 1956 this exciting personality, who was also the finest short-leg fielder in the game at this time, took 10 for 54 (16 for 83 in the match).

Right-arm fast-medium bowler Peter Loader's 9 for 17 against Warwickshire at The Oval in 1958 is another of the best performances ever to be seen in the Championship.

The stylish Peter May's contribution to this wonderful run of Championship wins can best be illustrated by pointing out that he topped Surrey's batting averages in all but one of the seven seasons, during which he hit 7832 runs (average 49·50) in the county competition.

I suppose it is significant that Surrey's astonishing run should have been ended by Yorkshire in 1959, in one of the most exciting Championship races ever seen. In the closing stages Surrey were still in with a chance of extending their winning run, but they were closely rivalled by Gloucestershire, Warwickshire and, of course, Yorkshire. The title was not decided until 1 September when, in one of the most thrilling finishes ever seen at Hove, Yorkshire were left to get 215 in 105 minutes. They hit everything in sight and won with seven minutes to spare.

As a matter of fact Surrey still beat Yorkshire both at home and away in 1959, but it was Yorkshire's fighting spirit which surprised most of the fans and won them the Championship outright for the first time in 14 years. Freddie Trueman took 92 wickets (average 18·60) this season and his penetrative bowling was the greatest personal contribution to this Yorkshire revival.

With the young side gaining experience, it was less of a surprise when Yorkshire carried off the title again the following season. However, although Yorkshire enjoyed another string of three wins in a row

Below left *Glenn Turner, a New Zealander who played county cricket for Worcestershire, drives backward of point*
Below right *Another overseas player to do well in the county championship, Sadiq Mohammad batting for Gloucestershire against Hampshire in 1978*

in the 1960s, recent seasons have been more notable from a cricket historian's point of view for the emergence of new powers in the competition.

Worcestershire not only won the Championship for the first time ever in 1964, but repeated the feat the following season and finished runners-up in the next campaign. This was quite an astonishing performance from a county whose previous best had been to finish runners-up in 1962 and way back in 1907. Worcestershire not only won the Championship for the first time in 1964 but won it by the widest margin in seven years. The margin was much closer in 1965 but it was particularly fitting that they should have carried off the title in this campaign as they were celebrating their centenary. They fully deserved the title with a run of 10 wins in their last 11 Championship matches.

The heroes of these two exciting Worcestershire seasons were batsmen Tom Graveney, who had been resurrected from Gloucestershire; West Indian Ron Headley, and, in the second of these two seasons, Basil d'Oliveria, the first non-white South African to appear in this competition. The majority of wickets were taken by the fast-medium bowlers, L. J. Coldwell and Jack Flavell, and the slow left-arm spinner, Norman Gifford. Coldwell took 8-38 v Surrey at Worcester in 1965, while in the previous Championship-winning campaign Flavell took 9-56 v Middlesex at Kidderminster. Gifford took 7-23 against Derbyshire at Chesterfield in 1965.

The other first-time winners in the period since Worcestershire came to the top have been Leicestershire in 1975 and, of course Essex in 1979.

Leicestershire's success was due more than anything to the shrewd and inspired captaincy of Ray Illingworth who had previously assisted his native Yorkshire to the Championship on seven occasions. They also had real depth of batting strength and spin-bowling of the highest-order. Barry Dudleston and John Steele enjoyed a first wicket partnership of 335 against Glamorgan at Leicester, while Ray Illingworth himself had the satisfaction of performing the hat-trick (against Surrey at The Oval) for the first time in his long and illustrious career.

The first Championship win by Essex in 1979 is of such recent vintage that no-one will need reminding of the remarkable part played by John Lever. There was one week in which he twice took 13 wickets in a match and he fairly dominated the fast bowlers in this year's campaign.

As previously mentioned only Northamptonshire, Somerset and Sussex have yet to win the Championship. While Northamptonshire have finished runners-up four times, and Sussex six times, it is

Below left
Determination on the face of bowler Ray Illingworth. After captaining Yorkshire to championship successes and England to an Ashes victory, he captained Leicestershire to their first championship success in 1975 – a splendid achievement.
Below Tom Graveney turns to leg. He left Gloucestershire to help Worcestershire to consecutive championship wins in 1964 and 1965

surprising, in view of such stars as Harold Gimblett, Bill Alley, L.C.H. Palairet, J.C. 'Farmer' White, and now Ian Botham, that Somerset have never finished higher than third (four times). Judging by their success in other competitions these past couple of seasons they seem like a good bet to break their Championship duck very soon. However, it is a long and strenuous competition which requires luck as well as skill and team spirit, and betting on the eventual winners is something to be avoided, especially in recent years, when there have been surprises.

Right *Despite bowlers like Tate and John Snow, seen here, and batsmen like Fry and Ranji, the best Sussex have managed in the championship is six times second*

Opposite above *Graham Gooch driving Knight of Surrey in the Benson and Hedges Cup Final of 1979, a first win in any major competition for Essex, which preceded a championship victory the same year.*

Opposite below *The main contributor to the victory of Essex in 1979 was John Lever, who took 26 championship wickets in one week.*

The Champion Counties since 1864 and Records for each County

The Champion County

1864 Surrey
1865 Nottinghamshire
1866 Middlesex
1867 Yorkshire
1868 Nottinghamshire
1869 Nottinghamshire and
      Yorkshire
1870 Yorkshire
1871 Nottinghamshire
1872 Nottinghamshire

The County Championship

1873 Nottinghamshire and
      Gloucestershire
1874 Gloucestershire
1875 Nottinghamshire
1876 Gloucestershire
1877 Gloucestershire
1878 Undecided
1879 Nottinghamshire
      and Lancashire
1880 Nottinghamshire
1881 Lancashire
1882 Nottinghamshire
      and Lancashire
1883 Nottinghamshire
1884 Nottinghamshire
1885 Nottinghamshire
1886 Nottinghamshire
1887 Surrey
1888 Surrey
1889 Nottinghamshire,
      Lancashire and Surrey
1890 Surrey
1891 Surrey
1892 Surrey
1893 Yorkshire

1894 Surrey
1895 Surrey
1896 Yorkshire
1897 Lancashire
1898 Yorkshire
1899 Surrey
1900 Yorkshire
1901 Yorkshire
1902 Yorkshire
1903 Middlesex
1904 Lancashire
1905 Yorkshire
1906 Kent
1907 Nottinghamshire
1908 Yorkshire
1909 Kent
1910 Kent
1911 Warwickshire
1912 Yorkshire
1913 Kent
1914 Surrey
1915–18 No competition
        owing to the war
1919 Yorkshire
1920 Middlesex
1921 Middlesex
1922 Yorkshire
1923 Yorkshire
1924 Yorkshire
1925 Yorkshire
1926 Lancashire
1927 Lancashire
1928 Lancashire
1929 Nottinghamshire
1930 Lancashire
1931 Yorkshire
1932 Yorkshire
1933 Yorkshire
1934 Lancashire
1935 Yorkshire
1936 Derbyshire

1937 Yorkshire
1938 Yorkshire
1939 Yorkshire
1940–45 No competition
        owing to the war
1946 Yorkshire
1947 Middlesex
1948 Glamorgan
1949 Middlesex and
      Yorkshire
1950 Lancashire and
      Surrey
1951 Warwickshire
1952 Surrey
1953 Surrey
1954 Surrey
1955 Surrey
1956 Surrey
1957 Surrey
1958 Surrey
1959 Yorkshire
1960 Yorkshire
1961 Hampshire
1962 Yorkshire
1963 Yorkshire
1964 Worcestershire
1965 Worcestershire
1966 Yorkshire
1967 Yorkshire
1968 Yorkshire
1969 Glamorgan
1970 Kent
1971 Surrey
1972 Warwickshire
1973 Hampshire
1974 Worcestershire
1975 Leicestershire
1976 Middlesex
1977 Middlesex and Kent
1978 Kent
1979 Essex

Derbyshire

Present club formed: 1870. Badge: Rose and crown. Colours: Chocolate, amber and pale blue. Ground: Nottingham Road, Derby, DE2 6DA. Honours: County Champions – 1936; Gillette Cup – finalists 1969; Benson and Hedges Cup – finalists 1978. Highest score for: 645 v Hampshire, at Derby, 1898. Highest score against: 662 by Yorkshire, at Chesterfield, 1898. Highest individual score for: 274 by G. Davidson v Lancashire, Manchester, 1896. Highest individual score against: 343 not out by P. Perrin of Essex, at Chesterfield, 1904. Lowest score for: 16 v Nottinghamshire, at Nottingham, 1879. Lowest score against: 23 by Hampshire, at Burton-on-Trent, 1958. Best innings bowling 10-40 by W. Bestwick v Glamorgan, at Cardiff, 1921.

Essex

Present club formed: 1876. Badge: three scimitars with word 'Essex' underneath. Colours: Blue, gold and red. Ground: The County Ground, New Writtle Street, Chelmsford, CM2 0RW. Honours: County Champions – 1979; Benson and Hedges – winners 1979; John Player League – runners-up 1971, 1976, 1977. Highest score for: 692 v Somerset, at Taunton, 1895. Highest score against: 803 for 4 declared by Kent, at Brentwood, 1934. Highest individual score for: 343 not out by P. Perrin v Derbyshire, at Chesterfield, 1904. Highest individual score against: 332 by W. H. Ashdown of Kent, at Brentwood, 1934. Lowest score for: 30 v Yorkshire, at Leyton, 1901. Lowest individual score against: 31 by Derbyshire, at Derby, 1914, and by Yorkshire, at Huddersfield, 1935. Best innings bowling: 10-32 by H. Pickett v Leicestershire, at Leyton, 1895.

First-ever trophy for Essex: Keith Fletcher holds the Benson and Hedges Cup aloft in 1979

Glamorgan

Present club formed: 1888. Badge: Gold daffodil. Colours: Blue and Gold. Ground: Sophia Gardens, Cardiff. Admitted to County Championship 1921. Honours: County Champions – 1948, 1969; Gillete Cup – finalists 1977. Highest score for: 587 for 8 declared v Derbyshire, at Cardiff, 1951. Highest score against: 653 for 6 declared by Gloucestershire, at Bristol, 1928. Highest individual score for: 287 not out by E. Davies v Gloucestershire, at Newport, 1939. Highest individual score against: 302 not out and 302 by W.R. Hammond of Gloucestershire, at Bristol, 1934, and Newport, 1939. Lowest score for: 22 v Lancashire, at Liverpool, 1924. (In Minor Counties Championship: 32 by Carmarthenshire, at Llanelly, 1910). Best innings bowling: 10-51 by J. Mercer v Worcestershire, at Worcester 1936.

Hampshire

Present club formed: 1863, re-organised 1879. Badge: Tudor rose and crown. Colours: Blue, gold and white. Ground: County Cricket Ground, Northlands Road, Southampton, SO9 2TY. Honours: County Champions – 1961, 1973; John Player League champions – 1975, 1978. Highest score for: 672 for 7 declared v Somerset, at Taunton, 1899. Highest score against: 742 by Surrey, at The Oval, 1909. Highest individual score for: 316 by R.H. Moore v Warwickshire, at Bournemouth, 1937. Highest individual score against: 302 not out by P. Holmes of Yorkshire, at Portsmouth, 1920. Lowest score for: 15 v Warwickshire, at Birmingham, 1922. Lowest score against: 23 by Yorkshire, at Middlesbrough, 1965. Best innings bowling: 9-25 by R.M.H. Cottam v Lancashire, at Manchester, 1965.

Gloucestershire

Present club formed: 1871. Badge: City and County of Bristol's coat of Arms. Colours: Blue, gold, brown, sky-blue, green and red. Ground: County Ground, Nevil Road, Bristol, BS7 9EJ. Honours: County Champions – 1873 (jointly with Nottinghamshire), 1874, 1876, 1877; Gillette Cup – winners 1973; Benson and Hedges Cup – winners 1977. Highest score for: 653 for 6 declared v Glamorgan, at Bristol, 1928. Highest score against: 774 for 7 declared by the Australians, at Bristol, 1948. In the County Championship: 607 by Nottinghamshire, at Bristol, 1899, and 607 for 6 declared by Kent, at Cheltenham, 1910. Highest individual score for; 318 not out by W.G. Grace v Yorkshire, at Cheltenham, 1876. Highest individual score against: 296 by A.O. Jones of Nottinghamshire, at Nottingham, 1903. Lowest score for : 17 v the Australians, at Cheltenham, 1896. In County Championship: 22 v Somerset, at Bristol, 1920. Lowest score against: 12 by Northamptonshire, at Gloucester, 1907. Best innings bowling: 10-40 by G. Dennett v Essex at Bristol, 1906.

Colin Blythe, who took ten wickets in an innings for Kent against Northamptonshire in 1907, the best innings performance by a Kent bowler

Kent

Present club formed: 1859, re-organised 1870. Badge: White horse on a red background. Colours: red and white. Ground: St. Lawrence Ground, Canterbury, CT1 3NZ. Honours: County Champions – 1906, 1909, 1910, 1913, 1970, 1977 (jointly with Middlesex), 1978. Gillete Cup – winners 1967, 1974, finalists 1971; John Player League Champions – 1972, 1973, 1976; Benson and Hedges Cup – winners 1973, 1976, 1978, finalists 1977. Highest score for: 803 for 4 declared v Essex, at Brentwood, 1934. Highest score against: 676 by the Australians, at Canterbury, 1921. In the County Championship – 627 for 9 declared by Worcestershire, at Worcester, 1905. Highest individual score for: 332 by W.H. Ashdown v Essex, at Brentwood, 1934. Highest individual score against: 334 by W.G. Grace for MCC, at Canterbury, 1876. Lowest score for: 18 v Sussex, at Gravesend, 1867 (one man absent). Lowest score against: 16 by Warwickshire, at Tonbridge, 1913. Best innings bowling: 10-30 by C. Blythe v Northamptonshire, at Northampton, 1907.

Lancashire

Present club formed: 1864. Badge: Red rose. Colours red, green and blue. Ground: Old Trafford, Manchester, M16 0PX. Honours: County Champions – 1879 (jointly with Nottinghamshire), 1881, 1882 (jointly with Nottinghamshire), 1889 (jointly with Nottinghamshire and Surrey), 1897, 1904, 1926, 1927, 1928, 1930, 1934, 1950 (jointly with Surrey); Gillette Cup – winners 1970, 1971, 1972, 1975, finalists 1974, 1976; John Player League Champions – 1969, 1970. Highest score for: 801 v Somerset, at Taunton, 1895. Highest score against: 634 by Surrey, at The Oval, 1898. Highest individual score for: 424 by A. C. MacLaren v Somerset, at Taunton, 1895. Highest individual score against: 315 not out by T. Hayward of Surrey, at The Oval, 1898. Lowest score for: 25 v Derbyshire, at Manchester, 1871. Lowest score against: 22 by Glamorgan, at Liverpool, 1924. Best innings bowling: 10-55 by J. Briggs v Worcestershire, at Manchester, 1900.

Leicestershire

Present club formed: 1879. Badge: a running fox, coloured gold, on a green background. Colours: Scarlet and dark green. Ground: County Ground, Grace Road, Leicester, LE2 8AD. Honours: County Champions – 1975; John Player League Champions – 1974, 1977; Benson and Hedges Cup – winners 1972, 1975, finalists 1974. Highest score for: 701 for 4 declared v Worcestershire, at Worcester, 1906. Highest score against: 739 for 7 declared by Nottinghamshire, at Nottingham, 1903. Highest individual score for: 252 not out by S. Coe v Northamptonshire, at Leicester, 1914. Highest individual score against: 341 by G. H. Hirst of Yorkshire, at Leicester, 1905. Lowest score for: 25 v Kent, at Leicester, 1912. Lowest score against: 24 by Glamorgan, at Leicester, 1971. Best innings bowling: 10-18 by G. Geary v Glamorgan, at Pontypridd, 1929.

Archie MacLaren of Lancashire, whose 424 against Somerset in 1895 is the highest score in the county championship

Middlesex

Present club formed: 1863. Badge: Three seaxes. Colours: Blue. Ground: Lord's Cricket Ground, St. John's Wood Road, London, NW8 8QN. Honours: County Champions 1866, 1903, 1920, 1921, 1947, 1949 (jointly with Yorkshire), 1976, 1977 (jointly with Kent): Gillette Cup – winners 1977, finalists 1975; Benson and Hedges Cup – finalists 1975. Highest score for: 642 for 3 declared v Hampshire, at Southampton, 1923. Highest score against: 665 by West Indies, at Lord's, 1939. In County Championship – 596 by Nottinghamshire, at Nottingham, 1887. Highest individual score for: 331 not out by J.D. Robertson v Worcestershire, at Worcester, 1949. Highest individual score against: 316 not out by J.B. Hobbs of Surrey, at Lord's, 1926. Lowest score for: 20 v MCC, at Lord's, 1864. In County Championship – 25 v Surrey, at the Oval, 1885. Lowest score against: 31 by Gloucestershire, at Bristol, 1924. Best innings bowling: 10-40 by G.O. Allen v Lancashire, at Lord's, 1929.

Northampton-shire

Present club formed: 1820, re-organised 1878. Badge: Tudor rose. Colours: Maroon. Ground: County Ground, Wantage Road, Northampton NN1 4TJ. Honours: County Champions – never: Gillette Cup – winners 1976, finalists 1979. Highest score for: 557 for 6 declared v Sussex at Hove, 1914. Highest score against: 670 for 9 declared by Sussex, at Hove, 1921. Highest individual score for: 300 by R. Subba Row v Surrey, at The Oval, 1958. Highest individual score against: 333 by K.S. Duleepsinhji of Sussex, at Hove, 1930. Lowest score for: 12 v Gloucestershire, at Gloucester, 1907. Lowest score against: 43 by Leicestershire, at Peterborough, 1968. Best innings bowling: 10-127 by V.W.C. Jupp v Kent, Tunbridge Wells, 1932.

Nottingham-shire

Present club formed: 1841, reorganised 1866. Badge: County badge of Nottinghamshire. Colours: Green and gold. Ground: County Cricket Ground, Trent Bridge, Nottingham NG2 6AG. Honours: County Champions – 1865, 1868, 1869 (jointly with Yorkshire), 1871, 1872, 1873 (jointly with Gloucestershire), 1875, 1879 (jointly with Lancashire), 1880, 1882 (jointly with Lancashire), 1883, 1884, 1885, 1886, 1889 (jointly with Lancashire and Surrey), 1907, 1929. Highest score for: 739 for 7 declared v Leicestershire, at Nottingham, 1903. Highest score against: 706 for 4 declared by Surrey at Nottingham, 1947. Highest individual score for: 312 not out by W.W. Keeton v Middlesex, at The Oval, 1939. Highest individual score against: 345 by C.G. Macartney, for the Australians, at Nottingham, 1921. In County Championship: 317 by W.R. Hammond of Gloucestershire, at Gloucester, 1936. Lowest score for: 13 v Yorkshire, at Nottingham, 1901. Lowest score against: 16 by Derbyshire, at Nottingham, 1879, and by Surrey, at The Oval, 1880. Best innings bowling: 10-66 by K. Smales v Gloucestershire, at Stroud, 1956.

Somerset

Present club formed: 1875. Badge: Wessex Wyvern. Colours: Black, white and maroon. Ground: County Cricket Ground, St. James's Street, Taunton, TA1 1JT. Honours: County Champions – never: Gillette Cup – winners 1979, finalists 1967, 1978; John Player League Champions – 1979. Highest score for: 675 for 9 declared v Hampshire, at Bath, 1924. Highest score against: 811 by Surrey, at The Oval, 1899. Highest individual score for: 310 by H. Gimblett v Sussex, at Eastbourne, 1948. Highest individual score against: 424 by A.C. MacLaren of Lancashire, at Taunton, 1895. Lowest score for: 25 v Gloucestershire, at Bristol, 1947. Lowest score against: 22 by Gloucestershire at Bristol, 1920. Best innings bowling: 10-49 by E.J. Tyler v Surrey, at Taunton, 1895.

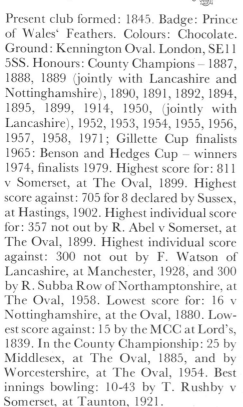

Joe Harstaff, whose father also played for Notts, batting against Middlesex in 1949. Leslie Compton is behind the wicket and Bill Edrich in the slips

Surrey

Present club formed: 1845. Badge: Prince of Wales' Feathers. Colours: Chocolate. Ground: Kennington Oval. London, SE11 5SS. Honours: County Champions – 1887, 1888, 1889 (jointly with Lancashire and Nottinghamshire), 1890, 1891, 1892, 1894, 1895, 1899, 1914, 1950, (jointly with Lancashire), 1952, 1953, 1954, 1955, 1956, 1957, 1958, 1971; Gillette Cup finalists 1965: Benson and Hedges Cup – winners 1974, finalists 1979. Highest score for: 811 v Somerset, at The Oval, 1899. Highest score against: 705 for 8 declared by Sussex, at Hastings, 1902. Highest individual score for: 357 not out by R. Abel v Somerset, at The Oval, 1899. Highest individual score against: 300 not out by F. Watson of Lancashire, at Manchester, 1928, and 300 by R. Subba Row of Northamptonshire, at The Oval, 1958. Lowest score for: 16 v Nottinghamshire, at the Oval, 1880. Lowest score against: 15 by the MCC at Lord's, 1839. In the County Championship: 25 by Middlesex, at The Oval, 1885, and by Worcestershire, at The Oval, 1954. Best innings bowling: 10-43 by T. Rushby v Somerset, at Taunton, 1921.

Sussex

Present club formed: 1839, reorganised 1857. Badge: County arms of six martlets. Colours: Dark blue, light blue and gold. Ground: County Ground, Eaton Road, Hove BN3 3AN. Honours: County Champions – never: Gillette Cup – winners 1963, 1964, 1978, finalists 1968, 1970, 1973. Highest score for: 705 for 8 declared v Surrey, at Hastings, 1902. Highest score against: 726 by Nottinghamshire, at Nottingham, 1895. Highest individual score for: 333 by K. S. Duleepsinhji v Northamptonshire, at Hove, 1930. Highest individual score against: 322 by E. Paynter of Lancashire, at Hove, 1937. Lowest score for: 19 v Surrey, at Godalming, 1830, and v Nottinghamshire (Sussex had one man absent), at Hove, 1873. Lowest score against: 18 by Kent (one man absent), at Gravesend, 1867. In County Championship: 35 by Kent, at Catford, 1894. Best innings bowling: 10-48 by C. H. G. Bland v Kent, at Tonbridge, 1899.

L. C. H. Palairet, one of Somerset's greatest players, a stylish batsman whose second innings against Yorkshire at Leeds in 1901 contributed to one of the most amazing turn-rounds in cricket history

Warwickshire

Present club formed: 1884. Badge: Bear and ragged staff. Colours: Blue, gold and silver. Ground: County Ground, Edgbaston, Birmingham, B5 7QU. Honours: County Champions – 1911, 1951, 1972: Gillette Cup – winners 1966, 1968: finalists 1964, 1972. Highest score for: 657 for 6 declared v Hampshire, at Birmingham, 1899. Highest score against: 887 by Yorkshire, at Birmingham, 1896. Highest individual score for: 305 not out by F. R. Foster v Worcestershire, at Birmingham, 1914. Highest individual score against: 316 by R. H. Moore of Hampshire, at Bournemouth, 1937. Lowest score for: 16 v Kent, at Tonbridge,

1913. Lowest score against: 15 by Hampshire, at Birmingham, 1922. Best innings bowling: 10-41 by J. D. Bannister v Combined Services, at Birmingham, 1959. In County Championship: 10-49 by W. E. Hollies v Nottinghamshire, at Birmingham, 1946.

Worcestershire

Present club formed: 1865. Badge: Shield, argent bearing fess between three pears sable. Colours: Dark green and black. Ground: County Ground, New Road, Worcestershire, WR2 4QQ. Honours: County Champions – 1964, 1965, 1974; Gillette Cup – finalists 1963, 1966: John Player League Champions – 1971; Benson and Hedges Cup – finalists 1973, 1976. Highest score for: 633 v Warwickshire, at Worcester, 1906. Highest score against: 701 for 4 declared by Leicestershire, at Worcester, 1906. Highest individual score for: 276 by F. L. Bowley v Hampshire, at Dudley, 1914. Highest individual score against: 331 not out by J. D. Robertson of Middlesex, at Worcester, 1949. Lowest score for: 24 v Yorkshire, at Huddersfield, 1903. Lowest score against: 30 by Hampshire, at Worcester, 1903. Best innings bowling: 9-23 by C. F. Root v Lancashire, at Worcester, 1931.

Yorkshire

Present club formed: 1863, reorganised 1891. Badge: White rose. Colours: Oxford blue, Cambridge blue and gold. Ground: Headingley Cricket Ground, Leeds, LS6 3BU. Honours: County Champions – 1867, 1869 (jointly with Nottinghamshire), 1870, 1893, 1896, 1898, 1900, 1901, 1902, 1905, 1908, 1912, 1919, 1922, 1923, 1924, 1925, 1931, 1932, 1933, 1935, 1937, 1938, 1939, 1946, 1949 (jointly with Middlesex), 1959, 1960, 1962, 1963, 1966, 1967, 1968; Gillette Cup – winners 1965, 1969. Benson and Hedges Cup – finalists 1972. Highest score for: 887 v Warwickshire, at Birmingham, 1896. Highest score against: 630 by Somerset, at Leeds, 1901. Highest individual score for: 341 by G. H. Hirst v Leicestershire, at Leicester, 1905. Highest individual score against: 318 not out by W. G. Grace of Gloucestershire, at Cheltenham, 1876. Lowest score for: 23 v Hampshire, at Middlesbrough, 1965. Lowest score against: 13 by Nottinghamshire, at Nottingham, 1901. Best innings bowling: 10-10 by H. Verity v Nottinghamshire, at Leeds, 1932.

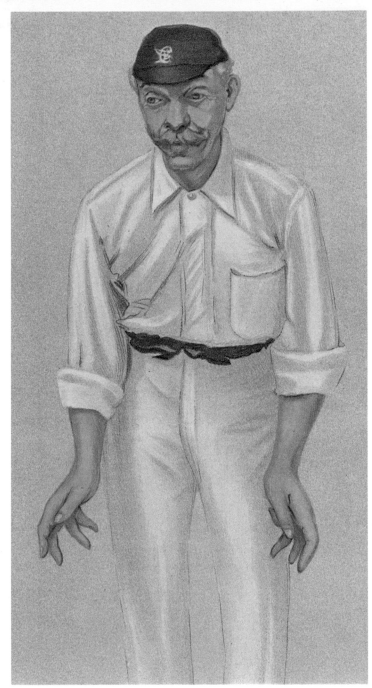

Bobby Abel, known as 'The Guvnor', whose 357 not out against Somerset in 1899 is the highest-ever for Surrey, who have been blessed with some of Emgland's greatest batsmen

The Golden Age of Cricket

Benny Green

The Golden Age is always behind us, which means that its location depends more on the eye of the beholder than it does on the age itself. However, if there is such a thing as a genuine Golden Age in English cricket history, then very powerful arguments exist to substantiate the theory that it ran roughly coeval with the Edwardian era. During this span, not only was there greatness in abundance, but there were so many varieties of greatness as to have tempted some commentators since to accept the cricket of the period as a witty microcosm of English society itself; certainly it is tempting to see the craggy pragmatism of Hirst and Rhodes as the personification of Yorkshire true grit, just as it is to observe the antics of milords Hawke and Harris and ascribe to them that patrician dottiness generally associated with the Emsworthian extravaganzas of P.G.Wodehouse.

If there really was a Golden Age, when exactly did it begin, and when did it die? Perhaps it gave notice of its arrival with the revolution in the structure of the County Championship in 1895, and perhaps it finally burst into glorious technicolour in 1900 with the parallel adjustment to the ritual of the game. For just as 1864 marks the end of cricket's Middle Ages, with the legalisation of over-arm bowling, W.G.Grace's first important century and the debut of Wisden's Cricketers' Almanack, so the acceptance as first-class counties in 1895 of Derbyshire, Essex, Hampshire, Leicestershire and Warwickshire, and the increase to six of the number

Above R. E. Foster, whose 287 for England at Sydney in 1903-04 is still the highest Test innings by an Englishman in Australia, had many relatives playing for 'Fostershire' or Worcestershire.
Right The England first innings in progress against Australia at Lord's in 1896. Eighty years on the policeman on the boundary would be told to sit down

of balls in an over, added the final refinements to a national structure already fully developed.

In every department of the game there was technical excellence expressed through quiddities of temperament often remarkable, and even bizarre. W.G. Grace, the embodiment of batting orthodoxy, sponsored the entry on to the international stage of the stupefying heresies of Gilbert Jessop. The Yorkshire bowler Peel nurtured the spinning fingers of his left hand on plentiful supplies of alcohol, a diet which eventually brought about his expulsion from the game by his captain, Lord Hawke, although the ironist has been savouring the joke ever since that Peel drunk was a better cricketer than Hawke sober. The schoolboys R.H. Spooner of Marlborough and J.N. Crawford of Repton lived out the adolescent fantasy of strolling from the sixth form straight into international acclaim. Records were established which have remained unbroken ever since, notably Charles Fry's six centuries in successive innings: R. E. Foster's 287 at Sydney, the highest test innings by any Englishman in Australia; and George Hirst's amazing double of two thousand runs and two hundred wickets in a season.

When asked if he thought anyone would ever equal his feat, Hirst is supposed to have replied, 'I don't know, but anyone who does will be very tired'. Much of this expertise was reflected in what might be called extra-sporting ways. Colin Blythe, the world's greatest left-arm slow bowler, soothed his own sensibilities by playing the violin; Arthur Shrewsbury, going out in the morning to open the innings, would be

Left *Lord Harris, an amateur and therefore a gentleman, and a powerful man in Edwardian cricket*
Right *Bobby Peel, a professional and therefore a player, and a good one, whether or not under the influence*

heard ordering a cup of tea to be sent out at four o'clock; Fry, no-balled for throwing, tried to reduce the umpire to a species of oblivion by bowling with a buttoned-down sleeve concealing the splint on his bowling arm; R.E. Foster's brother Basil divided his energies between playing for Worcestershire and appearing in 'The Merry Widow' at Daly's Theatre; the great Lancashire batsman J.T. Tyldesley attributed the prettiness of his footwork at the crease to the long winter evenings spent tripping the light fantastic in the arms of buxom Lancashire lasses. As a final refinement, English cricket had its own historian, H.S. Altham, its own statistician, F.S. Ashley-Cooper, even its own popular poetaster, Albert Craig. And perhaps most important of all, the period seemed to guarantee the continuance of its own tradition; by one of those whimsical coincidences in which the game seemed to specialise, in the match between Surrey and the Gentlemen of England at the Oval on Easter Monday, 24 April 1905, the captain of one side was W.G. Grace, the opening batsman for the other J.B. Hobbs, making his debut.

Reference to the 'Gentlemen of England' raises the vexed question of Class in English cricket. As it is generally assumed that a gentleman is someone who would never dream of advertising the fact, a designation like 'Gentlemen of England' is as ludicrous as a wink from a blind man. The official distinction in Edwardian cricket between the Gentleman and the Player was that the Gents played for love, the professionals for money. It is also true that George Eliot was one of the Bronte Sisters and that the moon is made of green cheese. It was an open secret that several amateurs, among them the England captain A.C. Maclaren, received more generous emoluments than many professionals, the only defence of this kind of hypocrisy being that at least its precedents were venerable; we learn that on the occasion of the 1877 Gloucestershire v Yorkshire match, the club secretary, Mr E. M. Grace, having decided that the event was 'a Grace testimonial game, raised the gate charge from 6d to one shilling without informing the committee'.

And yet the distinction, fraudulent though it may have been in the narrow juridical sense, was as inevitable as it was dishonest, for in dividing themselves into masters and servants, the cricketers of Edwardian England were merely reflecting the society of which they were a part, one which was sundered at every level by the distinctions between Lords and Commons, Officers and Other Ranks, Upstairs and Downstairs. There was even a sense in which the distinction was a real one, although its moral basis was laughable. A gentleman cricketer, whether or not he accepted payment, was someone who had been the beneficiary of what used laughingly to be described as the Higher Education, whose enunciation had been martyred at Oxbridge, whose table manners, sexual etiquette, habits of dress, financial expectations, though hardly more edifying than those of his brothers in the professional dressing room, were certainly different. It is perfectly true that a Bobby Peel or a Johnny Briggs would have been out of place at the high table of Lord Harris; what was insane was the conclusion which society drew from this distinction, which was that only the gentleman was fit to lead, whether in public life, witness Douglas Haig and Sir Edward Grey, or on the playing fields controlled by the likes of Lord Hawke, who, on one famous occasion, prayed to God that he would never live to see the day a professional led the

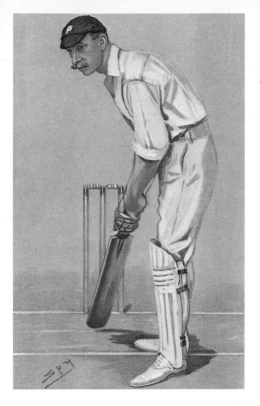

England side on to the field as captain.

The question of God is one which hangs like a pall over the cricket fields of Edwardian England. If the high noon of Victorian sanctimony was passing, there remained a strong intuition among sportsmen that God had dictated the rules of the MCC. Apart from Hawke's invocation to the Almighty regarding England team selection, and Lord Harris's definition of the cricket field as 'God's classroom', there was the touching case of Albert Knight, an orotund Leicestershire opening batsman whose habit of praying to God for assistance before receiving the first ball of the innings so incensed the Lancashire fast bowler Walter Brearley that he complained to the MCC. It is a nice point whose religious fervour was the more absolute, that of the professional Knight, who believed God would help him, or the amateur Brearley, who was so convinced he would as to construe the request as blatant cheating. Before a more godless age scoffs at this type of charade, it would do well to remember that cricket was still regarded by many as an adjunct of Christianity, and that 'just as freemasons referred to God as the Great Architect of the Universe, young cricketers were taught to think of Him as the One Great Scorer and

almost to regard a Straight Bat as second in religious symbolism only to the Cross of Jesus'. Both the Fosters and the Crawfords, among the most prolific brotherhoods in history, were fathered by reverend gentlemen.

Another aspect of the Golden Age reflecting the larger world was its imperial aspect. By the start of the century, Australian national sides were at least as strong as those of the Mother Country; South Africa was rapidly moving towards cricketing nationhood, and both the West Indies and India, suitably chaperoned by white administrators, were showing promise. The only colonial outpost where the game refused to flourish, and eventually withered, was Canada, in spite of the tour there in the 1870s by W.G. Grace. Elsewhere in the colonies, cricket was not only a game and a secular religion, but also an instrument of policy, and before the apologists for this system leap to its defence, it may be conceded instantly that history has known far blunter instruments of far crueller policies. Today, the modern schoolboy, bemused by requests to list the constituent parts of the old empire, has only to rattle off the names of the Test match playing countries to score himself full marks.

Top *J. T. Tyldesley,
best of the famous
Lancashire cricketing
brothers, an excellent
batsman on sticky
wickets*
Above *Tom Hayward,
whose record aggregate
for a season in 1906
stood until 1947. His
father and grandfather
also played for Surrey*

In fact, Edwardian cricket is a vivid world in miniature, the most beguiling Lilliput any social historian could wish to find. It reflected almost every nuance of the larger life it represented, and it is the essence of the achievement of one man, Sir Neville Cardus, that he was the first to perceive this and render it whole. In England at that time, character was still being expressed through those now discredited prisms, Class and County. The Yorkshireman Rhodes was as different in technique from the Kentishman Blythe as the Pennines from the chalk hills of the North Downs, and both were as alien to a contemporary like Pelham Warner as the Board school from Rugby. No two virtuosi of the Edwardian game were quite alike, and there are few archetypes they do not suggest as we imagine them running unknowing across the grass. Classicism was Tom Hayward, romanticism K.L. Hutchings. Jessop was pure melodrama, and C.B. Fry what Cardus somewhere defines as 'the dry light of ratiocination'. The eastern mysticism of Ranjitsinhji was balanced by the earthy genius of Tom Richardson, the quietism of Quaife by the fury of Kortright. Even those indispensable accoutrements of the Edwardian age, the seeds of Decadence, were being scattered by the all-rounder Bosanquet, whose hyper-sophisticated deceptions as a spin bowler, proving that after all nothing was what it seemed, were soon to render the front-foot heroics of the English amateur as quaint as a cavalry charge.

When did this Golden Age end, and what powers were they which broke it up? At what point did that compromise between technical resource and expression of temperament begin to disintegrate? One informed historian has suggested that in a game played in 1914 between the touring Philadelphians and Kent Club and Ground, the corpse of the Golden Age was finally laid to rest through the conduct of the Kent captain who, in order to avoid inevitable defeat, instructed his bowler to roll the last two deliveries of the match along the ground to prevent their being hit. While it is true that such behaviour verges on dementia, it is sentimentality of the worst kind to nominate so insignificant an occasion merely because of the resonance attaching to the figures 1914, and to imply thereby that until then all had been pristine. Gamesmanship and cheating had

been rampant ever since the first recorded cricket match, and it is interesting that the greatest ingenuity in this regard was usually displayed by the Gentlemen, who no doubt benefitted from that Higher Education of which they were so proud. Any lingering doubt that the Golden Age embraced deviousness as well as honour is dispelled by reference to the antics of the Cambridge side in the match against Oxford in 1893, when the captain, the Hon F.S. Jackson, instructed his bowlers to bowl wides in order to concede runs and avoid making their opponents follow on. Jackson subsequently became Chairman of the Conservative Party. What killed the Golden Age was, simply, what killed so much else, the Great War.

Posterity is forever tempted to seek for symbolic moments, and often elects as the perfect prelude for the entry into paradise the feats over a six-week period in 1899 of one Major Robert Montagu Poore, an officer in the British Army who, on returning from service in South Africa, joined the distinctly militaristic Hampshire side and scored seven centuries for them, including a treble century and two hundreds in one match, ending with an average of 116; had not the call of duty in the Boer War curtailed his cricket, there is no telling what he might not have done to the bowlers of England. But what is quintessentially Edwardian about Poore is the fact that cricket was only one of several activities pursued in those mercurial six weeks; during that time he played on the winning side in the final of the Inter-Regimental Polo championships and won the prize for the best Man-at-Arms at the Royal Tournament.

There remain at least two incidents of the Golden Age worthy of consideration, a mystery and a revelation. As to the mystery, it surrounds the burly figure of Edwin Boaler Alletson, an undistinguished Nottinghamshire all-rounder who for one brief afternoon in 1911 shrugged off his mediocrity to such violent effect that his performance has stood in the record books ever since as a reproach to subsequent, less elemental generations of cricketers. On Saturday 20 May, on the last day of the game with Sussex at Hove, Notts, trailing by 176 on the first innings, had lost seven for 185 in their second when Alletson, batting at number nine, walked out to bat and to contribute to the formality of a

Sussex victory. In the fifty minutes before lunch Alletson made 47 for the loss of two partners; after lunch the last Notts pair added another 152 runs in forty minutes, of which Alletson's share was 142; 89 of these were made in the last fifteen minutes. Nobody who witnessed the hurricane had ever seen anything like it before, nor ever would again. The mysterious aspect of the feat is that this most famous of all centuries in the history of the county championship was the only one Alletson made in his whole career.

The revelation may be found much earlier, at the start of the new century, in an incident which qualifies as cricket history only in the peripheral sense, although its significance can hardly be exaggerated. It lies concealed in the small print of Wisden, which reported a nondescript match played at Crystal Palace in May between W.G. Grace's London County side and a Surrey eleven. On the third day, Saturday 5 May, a touching pageant was enacted which hints at the degree to which the cricketers of the Golden Age, and Grace in particular, had achieved symbolic importance. A professional soldier called Sir George White, accompanied by his wife, drove on to the ground 'and had an enthusiastic reception'. This was the Sir George who had just recently performed one of the most renowned feats of arms in the history of warfare, his celebrated escape from Ladysmith after long months of insisting he wished to stay there. That a hero as celebrated as Sir George, at this apex of his career, on returning to a mother country he must have despaired of ever seeing again, should choose as one of his first public engagements, perhaps even the very first, to be presented to W.G. Grace on the field of play, is a fitting fact with which to close this argument in favour of the first years of this century as the Golden Age of English cricket. The anecdote is not only touching, not only historic, but also utterly appropriate, involving as it does the presence of an indisputably great national figure. I refer, of course, to Dr. Grace.

King George V at Lord's in 1914, talking to J. W. H. T. Douglas and C. B. Fry. Lord Hawke is with him. Behind the King is Prince Albert (later George VI) and the Prince of Wales, who is talking to Lord Harris

The Test Scene
Martin Tyler

In an era of one-day cricket's instant appeal, of the dictates of the sponsor, and of Kerry Packer, the most compelling day's cricket of 1979 came unquestionably in traditional surroundings.

Under the supreme guidance of Sunil Gavaskar's master batsmanship, India, with two wickets standing, fell gallantly just nine runs short of the 438 required for victory in the fourth Test match against England at the Oval. Three hundred and fifty-three of those runs were fashioned in captivating circumstances on the final day. Proof, and it may have been needed, that the game's highest pinnacle still offers the most satisfying fare to the genuine cricket lover.

Test cricket, indeed, was continuing into its second century in good health. The 1979-80 season offered a crammed schedule. Within a week of their heroics in London, the Indians were playing the first of 13 Tests within their own season, including another series in their revived contests against Pakistan. England and West Indies embarked upon tours of Australia, with the West Indians moving on to a further rubber in New Zealand.

Such a programme belongs exclusively to the jet-age, a facility denied those cricketers who became the first Test players. In 1877 James Lillywhite captained a troop of English professionals profitably engaged in showing off their skills in Australia. It was the fourth of such tours but finally the Australians were able to take on their opponents on equal terms. After a match against New South Wales, now

Sunil Gavaskar gets one past Hendrick during his 221 against England at The Oval, 1979

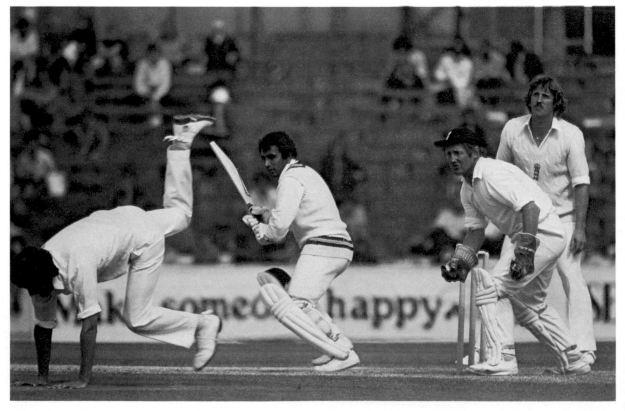

accepted as the initial first-class match between teams from the countries, an Australian XI met Lillywhite's side in Melbourne.

At the time there was no Test classification but when the meetings between the two countries were more formalised, this contest was retrospectively judged as the first Test. England's Alf Shaw bowled the first ball to Charles Bannerman, who became the first Test hero, making 165 before retiring hurt after a blow on the hand. Australia's 245 all out was the biggest total of the match and England, set 154 runs to win, were bowled out for 108. By a remarkable coincidence the Centenary Test of 1977 produced an identical result, a win for Australia by 45 runs.

The Australians had learned the game quickly and from these humble beginnings sprang the intense rivalry that is undiminished today. One further match ensured that the contest would have its own symbol. The first Test in England had taken place in 1880 at The Oval, where England, aided by W. G. Grace's 152, won by five wickets, but two years later Australia achieved momentous success.

England had not always fielded their best side in these early encounters but for

the only Test of 1882, on 28th and 29th August at the Oval, they had called upon all the cricketing giants in the land. Australia collapsed on the first morning and were finally dismissed for 63 but Spofforth's 7 for 46 restricted England's lead to 38. Though Australia again batted poorly in rain-affected conditions, one dismissal worked in their favour.

W. G. Grace was within the letter rather than the spirit of the Laws when he ran out S. P. Jones, who had forsaken his crease to prod down the divots on the pitch. Spofforth was incensed, and though England needed only 85 to win the 'Demon' was bent on revenge. England needed only 19 with five wickets left but lost by seven runs. Spofforth took his haul for the match to 14 for 90, figures that remained an Australian record against England until 1972.

The following day's *Sporting Times* recorded the much-recalled obituary notice: 'In affectionate Remembrance of English Cricket which died at the Oval......The body will be cremated and the Ashes taken to Australia.' The following year the charred remnants of a burnt stump were presented in an Urn to the Hon. Ivo Bligh whose team had won the rubber in

The Ashes urn

Derek Randall hooks Dennis Lillee for four in the Centenary Test at Melbourne in 1977

Above *Hobbs and Sutcliffe coming out to bat in the 1926 Test match at The Oval, when both scored centuries in a famous stand*
Opposite above *Bodyline in action. W. M. Woodfull ducks below a Harold Larwood bouncer in the Australia-England Test at Brisbane in 1933*
Opposite below *A wicket for Jim Laker. Clyde Walcott caught behind by Godfrey Evans as West Indies follow on, Trent Bridge, 1957*

cliff-hanger. Set 263 to win England slumped to 48 for 5, but Gloucestershire's Gilbert Jessop produced an incredible counter-attack. In 75 minutes he scored 104, and this time the last-wicket pair of Rhodes and George Hirst took the strain, picking off singles for the 15 needed for a thrilling victory.

England regained the Ashes in 1903-04 where the first Test produced a critical victory, largely on the strength of R. E. Foster's 287, a Test record at the time. But generally Australia, with great depth to their batting and penetrative pace and wrist-spin bowling, held the upper hand. Between 1920 and 1925 Australia won 12 of 15 Tests with only one England success.

In 1926, however, England recalled the 48-year old Rhodes and regained the Ashes at the Oval thanks to the genius of the opening partnership of Jack Hobbs and Herbert Sutcliffe, both of whom made centuries in conditions favourable to Australia's attack. But four years later the conveyor supply of raw talent produced another world-class Australian.

Arguably the greatest batsman of all time, Don Bradman announced himself to England in the 1930 series with scores of 8, 131, 254, 1, 334, 14, 232. His triple century came at Leeds, 309 on the first day: 105 before lunch, 115 in the afternoon and 89 after tea! In 52 Tests Bradman compiled 6996 runs, including 29 centuries, failing by 0·06 to average 100·00 when he was bowled second ball by Eric Hollies in his last Test innings at the Oval in 1948.

Largely as a result of Bradman's talent, Douglas Jardine, England's captain on the 1933-34 tour to Australia, conceived the 'bodyline' tactics that so outraged the Australians, and almost brought the series to an early conclusion. Harold Larwood and Bill Voce directed their attack at the batsman's body at a ferocious pace. Bradman made only one century as Larwood took 33 wickets and England took the series by four matches to one. But it was a highly controversial success and body line as such was discarded.

In 1938 Bradman had to watch at close-quarters as his record score was overhauled. The Ashes were already Australia's as Len Hutton, the 22-year old Yorkshire opener, batted for thirteen hours and twenty minutes to score 364. England totalled 903 for 7, still a Test record, and

Australia. Every series between England and Australia has subsequently been spiced by the battle for 'The Ashes'.

Indeed the contests between the two senior cricketing nations have provided much of Test history and folk-lore. The 1902 series in England typified much of the competitive sparkle of the early years. In the first of five Tests, Wilfred Rhodes took 7 for 17 as Australia plummetted to 36 all out, but they were saved by rain, which also washed out the second Test. At Sheffield, Australia won by 143 runs, setting up a fourth Test of triumph and tragedy.

The triumph came from Australian performances like Victor Trumper's century before lunch on the first morning; the tragedy surrounded Fred Tate, brother of Maurice. Tate dropped a vital catch in Australia's second innings, and was then summoned in at number 11 when England collapsed from 92 for 3 to 116 for 9, needing eight more to win. Tate hit his first ball for four but three balls later was bowled and Australia won by three runs.

Though the Ashes remained with Australia, the final Test produced another

with Bradman injured Australia were comfortably beaten by an innings.

If Hutton's achievement still shines out as the batting feat between the two countries, certainly the bowling achievement of all-time rests with another Yorkshireman. Jim Laker, though, fashioned his career with Surrey and in 1956 had already taken 10 for 88 in an innings for his county against the Australians by the time of the fourth Test at Old Trafford.

England, significantly, won the toss and Peter Richardson and the Reverend David Sheppard made centuries in a total of 459. On a dusty pitch Laker's off-spin took the first two wickets as Australia began their reply. His Surrey partner Tony Lock claimed the third but though Lock bowled 69 overs in helpful conditions it was, remarkably, to be his only success. Laker exerted a stranglehold over the Australians, who succumbed to a superb craftsman.

In the first innings his final analysis was 9 for 37; Australia 84 all out. In the second he took 10 for 53; England winners by an innings and 170 runs. His 19 wickets still remain as the most in any first class game, and Laker is still the only bowler to take ten

Above *Bob Massie's finest hour, the Lord's Test match of 1972. Ray Illingworth backs up as Massie bowls his way to 16 English wickets for 137 in the match*
Right *Geoff Miller, one of the all-rounders in England's successful side of the late 1970s*
Opposite *Alan Knott batting against Australia at Old Trafford in 1977, the last England-Australia series before the Kerry Packer intervention. Rodney Marsh is the wicketkeeper*

wickets in an innings in Test cricket. The Australians complained about the pitch, which particularly affected their first innings, but Laker's control and prodigious spin was immaculate. It is hard to conceive that his record will ever be beaten.

At Lord's in 1972 Bob Massie did come close. The strong Western Australian found atmospheric conditions perfectly suited to his ability to swing the ball both ways. Massie, who was to savour only a short career at the very highest level, claimed eight wickets in each innings to finish with match figures of 16 for 137.

The swapping of the Ashes continued throughout the 1970s with both sides enjoying periods of great supremacy. In 1974-75 the sheer pace of Dennis Lillee and Jeff Thomson brought Australia a crushing 4–1 success. Four years later, with Australia more than England hampered by the defection of the Packer players, Mike Brearley's closely-knit England side enjoyed their greatest success on foreign soil with a 5–1 victory in the series, despite Rodney Hogg's 41 wickets in his debut Test rubber.

Though tradition may find its richest vein in the annals of England-Australia

history books, Test cricket has expanded into a highly democratic concept. West Indies, India, New Zealand and Pakistan have all, at differing times, emerged from hesitancy to produce sides capable of success in the five-day game; also South Africa, until their ban from the International Cricket Conference in 1970.

South Africa, in fact, became the third Test playing country in 1889-90 when two matches (once more only labelled as Tests several years later) were played against a team of English players led by C. A. Smith, who was to find more lasting fame in Hollywood as Sir Charles Aubrey-Smith, actor. In the second game, Johnny Briggs took 7 for 17 and 8 for 11, fourteen of his victims cleaned bowled and the other falling leg before wicket. England won both matches in easy style.

South Africa's first Test triumph came in January 1906 in Johannesburg in fairytale fashion. England were again guilty of underestimating the development of their opponents and the party contained few front-line players. Once England had lost the first Test, when White and Sherwell were allowed to put on 48 for the last wicket to win the match, South African confidence blossomed. But it was 29 years before they won a Test in England.

Two Tests in South Africa are particularly worthy of recall. In 1938-39 the final Test was scheduled to be played to a finish with England leading the series by virtue of a win in Durban. Back on the same ground batsman on both sides took few risks in this 'timeless' match; Van der Byl batted for more than seven hours to make 125 in South Africa's first innings of 530. England replied with 316, while South Africa piled on the runs to set England 696 to win on a pitch that was kept intact by rain, which washed out the eighth day's play. With Gibb paving the way with a painstaking 120, Hammond scoring 140 and Edrich a splendid 219, England had reached 654 for 5 on the tenth day when rain intervened once more. But the players had to catch the boat home, so the match was abandoned as a draw.

Excitement of a more intense kind came in the 1948-49 series when in the first Test England won by two wickets from the game's very last ball, when Alec Bedser and Cliff Gladwin scrambled a leg bye. At the end of the same series England won again in the last breath of the match, when they successfully accepted the challenge of scoring 172 in 95 minutes to win, and lost seven wickets on the way.

South Africa first played Australia in a three-match series in 1902-03, but in the first 50 years of their meetings South Africa won only one Test, in 1911. Yet between 1952 and 1970 they beat Australia on ten occasions. In 1952-53 under the inspiring captaincy of Jack Cheetham they twice came from behind to square the series. In the fifth test at Melbourne a cavalier 76 from Roy McLean saw the visitors reach their target of 295 in the fourth innings.

However, the golden age of South African cricket was crammed into the last five years before their expulsion. Captained by Peter van der Merwe and later Ali Bacher, they produced great teamwork from a group of young and highly talented individuals. The batsmen were led by the competitive Eddie Barlow and classic Graeme Pollock, Bacher, himself, and the superb young Barry Richards. Peter Pollock's pace bowling found new support in Mike Procter, with the probing tenacity of the veteran all-rounder Trevor Goddard forever in support. Above all the fielding was of the highest class.

In 1965 South Africa won a three-match series in England, the one result being set up at Lord's by Graeme Pollock's 125 in 140 minutes while every other batsman was fumbling on a damp pitch. The two drawn games produced marvellous finishes, with England thwarted on the last day of the final match. Needing 91 in 70 minutes with six wickets in hand a thunderstorm put an end to the exhilaration. England have not played South Africa since that day.

In 1966-67 and 1969-70 Australia visited South Africa and were comprehensively beaten on both occasions. The first series belonged to wicket-keeper-batsman Denis Lindsay, who scored 606 runs, including three buccaneering centuries, and took 24 catches. South Africa won the first Test after Bobby Simpson's Australia had taken a first innings lead with only one wicket down and the host country never looked back, winning by three Tests to one. The rout was even more comprehensive when Bill Lawry's team provided the opposition, a 4–0 whitewash, with Richards making more than 500 runs in his only Test series and Procter claiming 26 wickets.

What followed is now one of the saddest chapters in recent cricket history. Had Basil D'Oliveira been an original selection for England's scheduled tour in 1968-69, the South African authorities would not have been given an easy solution for refusing to accept his membership of the England party. But political doctrine that stopped South Africa playing any Tests against West Indies, Pakistan and India would inevitably have been drawn into some other confrontation. The sporting tragedy is that the most talented generation of cricketers South Africa has ever produced were barred from displaying their talents at the highest levels.

The fourth nation to be accorded Test match status was West Indies, whose record on previous visits to England justified the upgrading that they received in 1928. England, who were to dominate their home series for some time won all three Tests by an innings, but when England visited the Caribbean in 1929-30 West Indies claimed their first victory after George Headley had made a century in both innings at Georgetown.

In their own islands the flamboyant cricket exhibited by West Indies has continually served them well but it was not until 1950 that they conquered their inhibitions overseas. In that series they

Opposite above *Rodney Hogg, the discovery of the Australian 1978-79 season, when he took 41 English Test wickets in his first series*
Opposite below *Kim Hughes on-driving. Hughes became Australia's captain while WSC cricketers were barred from Tests*

decimated England, and Sonny Ramadhin and Alf Valentine had calypsoes written about their mesmeric effect on the opposition. The two twenty-year-old spinners shared 59 wickets in the series: Valentine the bespectacled slow left-armer and Ramadhin, always bowling in a cap, purveying off-spin and leg-breaks with an almost identical action.

England won the first Test at Manchester but were destroyed at Lord's where Clyde Walcott struck 168 not out in the second innings to set up a massive victory by 326 runs. The two other 'W's, Frank Worrell and Everton Weekes, made centuries at Nottingham and West Indies won by ten wickets. Hutton had a personal triumph at The Oval, carrying his bat for 202 not out, yet England failed to save the follow-on and England were beaten by an innings.

England's bewilderment in the face of Ramadhin lasted until 1957, when Colin Cowdrey supported Peter May in a partnership that saved a match and won a series. Ramadhin had taken 7 for 49 in the first innings of the first Test and England trailed by 278. But May patiently created a recovery, batting for almost ten hours for

285, Cowdrey making 154. Ramadhin sent down 98 overs in the innings and lost his grip on England.

Since then it has been pace rather than guile which has been the main weapon in the West Indian armoury, with Wesley Hall, Charlie Griffith, Andy Roberts and Michael Holding the pick of a powerful battery of pace bowling through two decades. Hall and Griffith figured memorably in the marvellous Lord's Test of 1963 when Colin Cowdrey, nursing a broken arm, had to bat as partner to David Allen with two balls remaining and England a mere six runs short of victory.

In a rich array of superbly gifted players from the Caribbean Gary Sobers, now Sir Garfield, stands apart. In 93 Tests Sobers scored 8032 runs, the most in history, at an average of 57·78. With the new ball, with orthodox slow left-arm and with chinamen and googlies, he captured 235 wickets, plus 110 catches held in the most dexterous of hands. Such figures confirm Sobers as the greatest cricketer of modern times.

His record for the highest Test score, which is likely to remain unsurpassed for a long time, was incredibly his first century in Test cricket. At Kingston in 1958, in the third Test against Pakistan, he hit 38 fours in his 365 not out, taking three hours less than Hutton when he set the previous record. Sobers, however, would be the first to acknowledge that the circumstances were entirely different. Pakistan's attack was so depleted that they had only two fit regular bowlers; Conrad Hunte helped Sobers add 446 for the second wicket, before he was run out for 260.

West Indies first visited Australia in the 1930-31 series when the home team won the rubber by four matches to one. It was thirty years before the Australian public finally saw the best of West Indian cricket, and when they did they thronged the streets of Melbourne to say farewell to their visitors. It was an enthralling series which was won by Australia on the final day when they chased 258 to win at Melbourne and scrambled home by two wickets. But it was the first Test at Brisbane that set the tone for the series.

Australia faced a comfortable target at a comfortable pace, 233 to win at 45 runs an hour. At 92 for 6 they stared at seemingly certain defeat, but Alan Davidson, whose left-arm fast-medium bowling had set up the chance of victory, and Richie Benaud completely altered the balance of play. They had added 134 and needed only seven more for victory when Davidson was run out by a direct throw from Solomon. Wicket-keeper Wally Grout then took a single to set up a momentous last over from Wes Hall.

The fast bowler's long run was a useful tactical aid when West Indies wanted to use up time, and now it created added pressure on Australia. Grout acquired a leg bye from the first ball but off the second Benaud was caught behind the wicket. Ian Meckiff defended against the third, and from the fourth the two batsmen scampered a bye. Four balls left, four runs to win, two wickets left.

Below left Peter May, the England captain, batting at Edgbaston in 1957, where he scored 285 and finally overcame the mystery of Ramadhin
Below Gary Sobers, by common consent the greatest all-rounder seen in cricket, hooking for the Rest of the World team against England in 1970

A historic moment in cricket history: Australia v West Indies, Brisbane, 19 December 1960. Meckiff is run out on the penultimate ball of the final day, and cricket has its first tied Test

Hall's own composure was rattled when he dropped a high caught and bowled chance from the fifth delivery which brought Grout another run. Meckiff then swung the sixth ball high towards the leg-side boundary but charging in for a third run which would have won the game Grout was beaten by a superb throw from Hunte. Lindsay Kline, the last man, entered the fray with two balls remaining and the scores level. Kline pushed his first ball out on the leg side but Meckiff was run out when Solomon, with one stump to aim at, hit the target. It was the first Test match to finish in a tie.

At the same time that one England side was touring the West Indies in 1929-30, another, under the leadership of A. H. H. Gilligan, played four Tests in New Zealand, thus bringing the number of Test-playing nations up to five. Maurice Allom, bowling for the first time in a Test match, took four wickets in five balls including the hat-trick in the first meeting, which England won by eight wickets. The other three Tests were drawn.

The lack of professionalism in New Zealand cricket has always restricted their impact at the highest level, though individuals like John Reid, Bert Sutcliffe, Martin Donnelly and more recently Glenn Turner, Geoff Howarth and Richard Hadlee have exhibited great ability in the Test arena.

New Zealand, in fact, had to wait 26 years for their first Test victory, which arrived on 13 March 1956 at Eden Park, Auckland. Reid struck 84, the top score of the match, against a West Indies attack that included Ramadhin and Valentine, and the 19-year old Sobers. West Indies collapsed to 77 all out in their second innings and New Zealand broke their duck with a win by 190 runs.

Since then they have achieved victories over all the other Test playing countries, and have subsequently earned their right to a full participation at Test level. Their much-awaited first triumph over England arrived in the 48th Test between the two countries, 48 years after the first. Under the captaincy of Geoff Boycott, England trailed by only 13 on first innings in a low-scoring match played in gale-force conditions in Wellington.

When New Zealand collapsed before Bob Willis from 82 for 1 to 123 all out the home country faced apparent defeat once more. But they drew great resolution from the dismissal of Boycott in the second over and only Botham, 19, and Edmonds, 11, reached double figures. Superbly aggressive bowling by Richard Hadlee, 6 for 26, reinforced by splendid catching, reduced England to 64 all out. For New Zealand, who had suffered great indignities in the past, including being bowled out for 26 at Auckland in 1955, the lowest-ever Test score, it was a moment of sweet revenge.

Though there had been cricketing contact between England and India in the 19th century it was not until 1932 that the first Test match was played between the two nations. Like New Zealand, India have not consistently produced sides of the highest class, though in their own country their spinners, particularly Chandrasekhar, Bedi, Prasanna and Venkataraghavan of recent vintage have severely examined the best players in the world. Abroad their inability to unearth bowling of any pace has proved a great handicap and at times their performances have depended on individual heroics.

India's most revered hero in this respect was Vinoo Mankad, who, in a losing side, achieved the double of 1000 runs and 100 wickets in only 23 Tests. In Madras in 1952, when India achieved their first success over England, he had match figures of 12 for 108. Only months later he again played magnificently in a series in England when India were in danger of disappearing without trace when confronted by the blistering pace of the youthful Fred Trueman; at Headingly in the first Test the Indian second innings scoreboard infamously registered nought for four wickets. But at Lord's Mankad scored 72 and 184 and in England's first innings shouldered 73 overs, taking 5 for 196.

Mankad's name remains in the record books for his share in the biggest first-wicket partnership in Test history, 413 with Pankaj Roy at Madras against New Zealand in the 1955-56 series. Mankad was finally dismissed for 231.

In the 1970s, Sunil Gavaskar has added his name to the list of genuine world-class Indian players. In 1971 in the West Indies he amassed 774 runs at an average of 154·80 as India won the series with the only victory, in Trinidad. Gavaskar played a major part in another famous victory, also in Port-of-Spain, five years later, when India scored 406 for 4 in the fourth innings. Gavaskar's 102 and Viswanath's 112 were at the core of the triumph, and it should really have come as no surprise that India were able to get so close to a similar target at The Oval in 1979.

But later in the 1975–76 series in the West Indies, India's sometimes suspect and brittle temperament reached the surface again. In an apparent protest against the over-use of the bouncer by the West Indies' attack Bishan Bedi ended his side's second innings at 97 for 5, leaving the West Indies only 13 runs to win. Later it was revealed that five Indians were unfit to bat, and the innings has been recorded as being complete.

The partition in the sub-continent enabled Pakistan's membership to the Imperial Cricket Conference to be approved in 1952. A. H. Kardar, who had played for India as Abdul Hafeez, captained Pakistan's first excursion into Test cricket, a five-match rubber in India in 1952-53. Seventeen-year old Hanif Mohammed, the most renowned of five brothers who appeared in first-class cricket, played in all five games.

In 1979 India at last found an opening bowler of pace and control. Kapil Dev was their most successful bowler in the series in England.

Above *Ian Botham in typical belligerent style scattering the close field on his way to 108 in the second Test against Pakistan at Lord's, 1978*
Right *Lawrence Rowe, the only batsman to score a double century and a century in his Test debut*

India won the first Test by an innings, but Pakistan reversed the result at Lucknow for their initial international success, Fazal Mahmood, of whom more in a moment, finishing with match figures of 12 for 94. India clinched the rubber with a win at Bombay and the series ended with two drawn games – results that began a run of 13 successive draws between the two nations, including what is generally regarded as the most tedious of all series in 1954-55. After another unimaginative series in 1960-61, the two nations, amidst political turmoil, did not play each other again until October 1978, when Pakistan won a three–match series 2–0.

Pakistan, however, soon earned their spurs in a wider sphere when in 1954 they became the first country to win a Test match on a first tour of England. Their success came at the Oval at the end of a four-match series which England led through a win by an innings at Trent Bridge where Denis Compton struck 278; the other two Tests had been casualties of a frustratingly wet summer.

For the final match England chose to rest Alec Bedser, who had carried the attack on his broad shoulders for much of the post-war era, and Trevor Bailey, and with a dispute over the captaincy between the claims of the professional, Hutton, and the amateur, Sheppard, there was a feeling of uneasiness about the party.

Rain was in the South London air for most of the low-scoring match and Bedser was badly missed. Even so, England, at 109 for 2, needing 168 to win, appeared to have survived. But Fazal Mahmood, medium-fast in the Bedser style, put his name on the match. In the first innings he had captured six for 53, and now he sent England tumbling to 143 all out and defeat by 24 runs. Fazal's match analysis read 12 for 99.

Fazal's artistry shone through Pakistan's first Test against Australia in 1956. Ian Johnson's side were on their way home from their tour of England and one match was played on a matting wicket in Karachi. On the first day only 95 runs were scored, but in enthralling circumstances: Australia 80 all out, Pakistan 15 for 2. Fazal's craftsmanship dominated the play, as he claimed the first 6 wickets for 26 in sixteen overs, finishing with 6 for 34, figures he bettered in the second innings with 7 for 80. Pakistan needed only 69 runs for victory, though it took them one ball less than 49 overs to reach their target.

Outside the context of great Test matches there have been marvellous individual achievements like that of Lawrence Rowe who marked his Test debut by scoring 214 and 100 not out for West Indies against New Zealand at Kingston in 1971-72, the only batsman in Test history to accomplish such feat; like Clyde Walcott, who in the 1954-55 series between West Indies scored a century in both innings of two Test matches; like Vivian Richards, who in the calendar year of 1976 amassed 1710 Test runs, including a massive 291 against England at The Oval; like Jack Gregory, who struck the fastest hundred in Test cricket for Australia against South Africa in 1921-22 in a mere 70 minutes; like Bill Ponsford and Don Bradman, who put on 451 for the second Australian wicket against England at The Oval in 1934, the highest partnership in Test cricket.

New altitudes are, of course being reached all the time as 23-year-old Ian Botham proved in 1979. The combative Somerset all-rounder overtook Mankad when he achieved the double of 1000 runs and 100 wickets in only his 21st Test. He achieved his bowling target in characteristic style by out-thinking his most obdurate opponent of the series, Gavaskar, and the thousandth run came from a thumping boundary which typified his lack of inhibitions with the bat.

Lance Gibbs holds the record for the most Test wickets, 309. The long-fingered off-spinner edged ahead of Fred Trueman in his 79th and last Test of an international career that spanned 18 years. Trueman's striking rate was more spectacular, his 307 wickets coming in only 67 Tests, and he bowled some twelve thousand deliveries less than Gibbs. The Yorkshireman was first past the 300 mark in dramatic circumstances in 1964.

Then 33 years old, he was dropped for the fourth Test against Australia with his tally on 297, and it seemed possible that his Test career was over. Even when he was recalled for the final Test at The Oval his opening spell did little to suggest that the landmark would be reached. But digging deep into his resources, he shot out Ian Redpath and Graham McKenzie with successive deliveries. The coup de grace finally arrived by courtesy of a slip catch by

Milestone for Fred Trueman, the first man to capture 300 Test wickets. This is the 300th: Neil Hawke caught by Cowdrey at first slip, The Oval, 15 August 1964. Parfitt is at second slip and Parks behind the wicket

Colin Cowdrey; the victim was Trueman's long time friend Neil Hawke.

Sydney Barnes, who played so much of his cricket in the Minor Counties for Staffordshire, holds the record for most wickets in a Test series, set back in 1913–14 when he exerted such control over the South Africans that he captured 49 wickets despite missing the last match. At Johannesburg his mastery was almost total as 17 wickets tumbled to his brisk medium-pace for 159 runs, match figures that remain second only to those of Laker at Manchester in 1956.

Test hat-tricks have been understandably rare events, only 17 to the start of the 1979 season, notably those of Maurice Allom and New Zealand's Peter Petherick (against Pakistan in 1976-77) on their Test debuts, by Geoff Griffin of South Africa at Lords in 1960 in the same match in which he was no-balled for throwing, and by T. J. Matthews for Australia against South Africa at Manchester in the Triangular Tournament of 1912. Matthews did the hat-trick in each innings, a unique feat in Test cricket, and remarkably those six wickets were his only victims in the match!

Alan Knott, at the time of writing, leads the wicket-keepers with 252 Test victims in 89 Tests, including 233 catches, another Test record and a tribute to the quality of the pace bowling in the England side during his period of tenure. Australia's Rodney Marsh enjoyed a similar advantage, and before he joined up with Kerry Packer he had snared 198 victims in only 52 Tests, including 26 all caught in a six-match series against the West Indies in 1975-76, a mark shared with John Waite, the tall South African, whose achievement included three stumpings against New Zealand in 1961-62.

The Test cricketer of the 1980s travels the world by jet, is well rewarded for his efforts, thanks to sponsorship, by most of the major countries, and usually bats in a helmet. His efforts are captured by television, and recorded by large numbers of pressmen, one of whom might be enlisted for help with his 'autobiography', and a corps of statisticians. But in one important aspect he remains identical to his counterparts in decades gone by.

He is a representative of his country in the purest form of his sport. Test cricket still produces the definitive contest between bat and ball, and that is why it survived the challenge of Kerry Packer. And that is why for all the heady champagne of the second World Cup competition, the innings of 1979 was played on a bright Tuesday in September by Sunil Gavaskar!

Out! Trent Bridge 1977: Boycott called, Randall ran and Marsh made a mess of the wicket

England were very successful in Australia in 1978-79, winning the Test series 5-1. At Sydney, Higgs is lbw to Embury as the close field appeals

A Gallery of Great Players
Maurice Golesworthy

The great Syd Barnes, who over the course of 40 years or so reckoned to get a wicket for every eight runs scored from him

Barnes, Sydney Francis

There is no doubt that Syd Barnes, a marvel from Staffordshire, was the greatest Test bowler of all time. The astonishing fact is that he played only a small number of first-class games, for he spent most of his career in League cricket or with Staffordshire among the Minor Counties. His first-class appearances in County cricket were with Warwickshire 1894-96, and with Lancashire 1899-1903. A fast-medium bowler he first appeared for England in 1902, and when he made the last of his 27 Test appearances in 1914 he had maintained a remarkable average of seven wickets per Test at a cost of only 16·43 runs apiece. Sydney Barnes continued to bowl until he was 57 years of age and it has been calculated that in all classes of cricket he captured over 6000 wickets at an astonishing average of a little over eight runs each. In South Africa in 1913-14 he created a record for any Test series by taking 49 wickets.

Born 19 April, 1873, at Smethwick, Staffs. Died December 26, 1967, at Cannock, Staffs. Career aggregate of wickets (1895-1914): 719 (average 17·09). 27 England Tests – 189 wickets (average 16·43). Best bowling: 9-103 v South Africa, Johannesburg, 1913-14.

Bedi, Bishan Singh

India has produced many fine spin bowlers but none greater than Bishan Bedi, who so delighted the fans in England during his six seasons (1972-77) with Northamptonshire. A left-arm spinner who likes to keep on the attack rather than bowl defensively, he has taken more Test wickets than any other bowler for India, and, indeed, his total of 266 has only been exceeded by Gibbs and Trueman. Bedi was only 15 years of age when he made his first-class debut for Northern Punjab in the Ranji Trophy in 1961-62 and his Test debut was against the West Indies at Calcutta in January 1967. Since 1968 he has played for Delhi. Quite apart from his accurate bowling his beard and turban made him an outstanding figure in English cricket during his spell with Northamptonshire, and when they finished third in the Championship in 1973 he was the leading wicket-taker in the country with 105 (average 17·94). To the end of 1979 he had captained India in 22 Tests before being succeeded by Sunil Gavaskar. His most successful Test series was that against Australia in 1977-78 when he captured 31 wickets (average 23·87).

Born 25 September 1946 at Amritsar, India. Career aggregate of wickets (1961-79): 1507 (average 21·71). Best bowling: 7-5 (13-34 in the match), Delhi v Jammu and Kashmir, Delhi, 1974-75. 67 Tests – 266 wickets (average 28·70) Best Test bowling: 7-98 v Australia, Calcutta, 1969-70.

Bedser, Alec Victor

Alec Bedser was a great-hearted bowler who made one of the finest Test debuts ever when he appeared against India at Lord's in 1946: 7 for 49 and 4 for 96. Just to prove this was not beginner's luck he equalled this in his next Test with 4 for 41 and 7 for 52. A right-arm medium-fast bowler his total of 236 Test wickets at an average cost of 24·89 makes him one of England's most

economical bowlers. One of cricketing twins, Alec made his debut for Surrey in 1939 and remained with them until his retirement in 1960. He was appointed a Test selector in 1962 and has been Chairman since 1969. He took 100 wickets in a season 11 times, his best being 162 in 1953. It was in that summer that he captured 39 Australian Test wickets (average 17·48). Only Laker has taken more Australian wickets in a Test series.

Born 4 July 1918 at Reading, Berkshire. Career aggregate of wickets: 1924 (average 20·41). Best bowling: 8-18 v Notts, Oval, 1952, and 8-18 v Warwicks, Oval, 1953. 51 Tests – 236 wickets (average 24·89). Best Test bowling: 7-55 and 7-44 v Australia, Trent Bridge, 1953.

Benaud, Richie

All-rounder Richie Benaud is the man who put the fighting heart back into Australian cricket when first given the job as captain in 1958. He recaptured the Ashes in the 1958-59 series, then led them to victory against Pakistan, India and the West Indies, as well as retaining the Ashes in England in 1961 and at home in 1962-63. A real competitor whether batting, bowling, fielding or as captain, this exciting player was especially noted as a leg-break bowler. He took more Test wickets than any other Australian, and one of his finest all-round performances was that against South Africa, at Johannesburg, in 1957-58. In the fourth Test he scored 100 and followed this by taking 4-70 and 5-84. Benaud played for New South Wales throughout his first-class career and captained them from 1958 to 1963. No man ever enjoyed his cricket more.

Born 6 October 1930, at Penrith, New South Wales. Career aggregates (1948-63): 11432 runs (average 36·29); 935 wickets (average 24·80). 63 Tests – 2,201 runs (average 24·45); 248 wickets (average 27·03). Highest score: 187 v Natal, Pietermaritzburg, 1957-58. Best bowling: 7-32 New South Wales v Victoria, Melbourne, 1958-59.

Alec Bedser was England's best bowler from the end of the Second World War to the mid-1950s, during which time he took 236 Test wickets

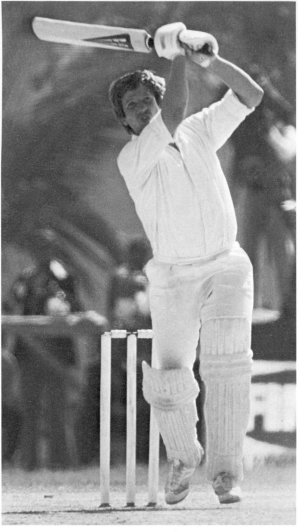

Above *India's Bishan Bedi delighted cricket fans everywhere with his slow bowling, and his 266 Test wickets are no more than his skill deserves*

Above right
Aggression rather than guile is Ian Botham's style, but nobody with 1 000 Test runs and 100 Test wickets is without considerable aptitude and technique. The picture is from the Pakistan tour of 1977-78

Botham, Ian Terence

This most determined and athletic of cricketers Ian Botham burst upon the Test scene when he set England on the path to victory by taking five Australian wickets for 74 runs in the first innings of the third Test of 1977. At one point he had taken four for 13 in 34 balls. We may wonder now how many spectators at Nottingham realised that a new international star had been born. He was one of *Wisden's* 'Cricketers of the Year' that summer and in the following year against Pakistan, at Lord's, he became the first player ever to score a century (108) and take eight wickets in a Test innings (8-34). Almost as exciting a batsman as he is a fast-medium bowler, this aggressive player created a new record by reaching a Test double of 1000 runs and 100 wickets in only 21 matches. Botham made his debut for Somerset in 1974 and is one of the most versatile bowlers on the scene today, swinging the ball both ways. His skill and enthusiasm have proved infectious in the Somerset and England teams, and he joined the England selection squad in Australia in 1979-80.

Born 24 November 1955, at Heswall, Cheshire. Career aggregates (1974-79) – 4 812 runs (average 28·71); 471 wickets (average 22·92). 21 Tests – 1 035 runs (average 38·33); 107 wickets (average 19·60). Highest score: 167 v Notts, Nottingham. Highest Test score: 137 v India, Leeds, 1979. Best Test bowling: 8-34 v Pakistan, Lord's, 1978.

Boycott, Geoffrey

Geoffrey Boycott did not set out to become the most popular personality in the game but the most technically perfect batsman. Despite the controversy that has surrounded him his popular image has recently improved, but that improvement does not compare with the stature he has achieved as one of the world's finest batsmen. A most determined player his rise to fame was meteoric. He made his first-class debut for Yorkshire in 1962 and in 1964 opened for England in the first Test against Australia. After 63 Tests he declined an invitation to tour Australia in 1974-75 stating that he no longer wished to play for England. His absence ended in 1977 when he returned to make 107 and 80 not out against Australia at Trent Bridge and then had his Yorkshire fans in raptures by scoring his hundredth century (191) in the next Test at Leeds. Boycott, who plays in contact lenses, has often been criticised for slow scoring, but he is the only English batsman ever to have averaged 100 in a season – 100·12 in 1971 and 102·53 in 1979.

Born 21 October 1940 at Fitzwilliam, nr Pontefract, Yorkshire. Career aggregate runs (1962-79): 35761 (average 56·94). Highest score: 261 not out for MCC v President's XI, Bridgetown, 1973-74. 83 Tests – 6090 runs (average 48·71). Highest Test score: 246 not out v India, Leeds, 1967.

Geoffrey Boycott, modern cricket's most dedicated run-gatherer, whose devotion to averages has resulted in the only two averages of over a hundred for a season to be recorded by an English batsman

Don Bradman, the most successful batsman in the history of the game, completes 2 500 runs for the season by turning Larwood to the boundary in The Oval Test of 1930. Duckworth is the wicket-keeper

Bradman, Sir Donald George

While Don Bradman's batting style may not have pleased the purists there is no denying that this Australian was the finest run-scoring machine ever seen. 'Machine' is a reasonable word to describe Bradman, for he was a cold, calculating batting genius with almost inhuman powers of concentration and endurance. Figures can be used to prove anything but one only has to quote this player's Test average to dispel any thoughts that superlatives used to describe his scoring powers may be exaggerated. That figure is 99·94 in 52 matches! Bradman's displays of run-getting are legendary. Among them is the innings of 334 against England at Leeds in 1930. This was not only the highest Test score but included a century (105) before lunch on the first day (one of only four such centuries in Tests) and a total of 309 not out at the end of that day, which is the highest individual Test score in a single day's play.

Born 27 August 1908, at Cootamundra, New South Wales. Career aggregate runs (1927-49): 28067 (average 95·14). Highest score: 452 not out for New South Wales v Queensland, Sydney, 1929-30. 52 Tests—6996 runs (average 99·94). Highest Test score: 334 (as above).

the age of 20 years 19 days he made 102 against Australia at Trent Bridge. Probably the most thrilling of his many scintillating displays was his 300 in 181 minutes for the MCC against N E Transvaal, at Benoni, in December 1948. 198 of those runs were from boundary hits and it was the fastest triple century on record.

Denis Compton and his brother Leslie, who also played for Middlesex, were accomplished footballers with Arsenal. Leslie gained an England cap, but Denis's appearances for England were during the war, and do not count as full internationals.

Born 23 May 1918, at Hendon, Middlesex. Career aggregate runs (1936-64): 38942 (average 51·85). Highest score: 300 (as above). 78 Tests – 5807 runs (average 50·06). Highest Test score: 276 v Pakistan, Trent Bridge, 1954.

Denis Compton jumps out and drives high. It was Denis's style as much as his record scoring that ensured his place in the game

Compton, Denis Charles Scott

Any mention of Denis Compton brings to mind that glorious summer of 1947 when he played some of the most entertaining and exhilarating cricket ever seen, and created a record by scoring 3816 runs (average 90·85). During that remarkable campaign he hit a record number of 18 centuries, his highest being 246 for Middlesex v The Rest, at the Oval. This daring batsman began with Middlesex in 1936 and made his Test debut as a 19-year-old against New Zealand the following year. In 1938 he became the youngest player ever to score a Test century when at

Cowdrey, Michael Colin

A classy Kent batsman, who also captained England 27 times, Colin Cowdrey has appeared in more Tests than any other player, and only Gary Sobers has scored more Test runs. Cowdrey played his cricket in the grand manner, but there were times when his *sang froid* irritated some of his critics who believed that he needed more of the killer instinct. However, he usually delighted the fans with some of the most effortless batting ever seen. In 114 Tests he shared in 41 century partnerships. His batting technique was of text book perfection and one of his best remembered innings was against the West Indies at Edgbaston in 1957 when he and Peter May put on 411 in 8 hours 20 minutes. Cowdrey was the first man to score a century in each innings of a match in England against the Australians: 149 and 121 at Canterbury in 1961.

Born 24 December 1932, at Bangalore, India. Career aggregate runs (1950-76); 42719 (average 42·89). Highest score: 307 MCC v S Australia, Adelaide, 1962-63. 114 Tests – 7624 runs (average 44·06). Highest Test score: 182 v Pakistan, Oval, 1962.

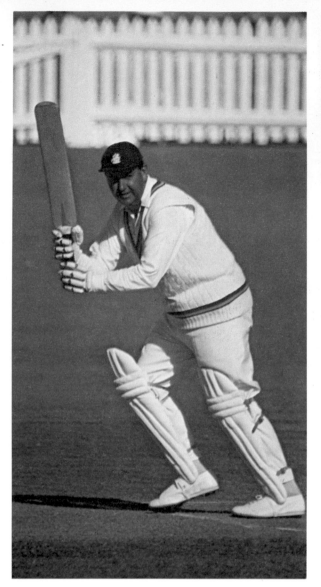

Above Colin Cowdrey played in 114 Tests – more than any other player – and only Gary Sobers scored more Test runs

Above right Lance Gibbs has more Test wickets than any man: 309, spread over a Test career lasting 20 years

Freeman, Alfred Percy

'Tich' Freeman (he stood only 5 ft 2 in tall) was one of the world's finest spin bowlers for a period of about 15 years after the First World War. Maybe he did not do himself justice in Test cricket, but for Kent in the County Championship he reigned supreme among leg-break bowlers. Only Wilf Rhodes exceeded this player's career aggregate of wickets, and Freeman's best two seasons rank first and second among bowlers with most wickets in a single campaign: 304 in 1928 and 298 in 1933. He took over 200 wickets in a season no less than seven times! At Hove in 1922 he took nine Sussex wickets in only 47 balls for 11 runs and completed the match with 17 for 67. He also took 17 wickets for 92 against Warwickshire at Folkestone in 1932. During his career he performed the hat-trick three times, and took ten wickets in an innings three times.

Born 17 May 1888, at Lewisham, London. Died 28 January 1965, at Bearsted, Kent. Career aggregate wickets (1914-36): 3,776 (average 18·42). Best bowling (innings) 10-53 Kent v Essex, Southend, 1930. 12 Tests – 66 wickets (average 25·86), Best Test bowling: 7-71 v South Africa, Old Trafford, 1929.

Gibbs, Richard Lancelot

Lance Gibbs began as a leg-break bowler in his native Guyana and developed into one of the greatest off-spinners of all time, taking more Test wickets than any other player in the game's history. He made his Test debut for the West Indies against Pakistan in 1957, and after a spell around 1970 when he was thought to be finished with top class cricket he came back with one of his finest series against Australia in 1972-73, capturing 26 wickets (average 26·76). He then continued as a Test player until 1975-76 when against Australia he passed Fred Trueman's record of Test wickets. Prior to 1972-73 his finest Test series was that against England in 1963 when he also took 26 wickets (average 21·30). In 1960-61 he became the first man this century to perform a hat-trick in Australia. He had seven seasons with Warwickshire from 1967 and helped them win the Championship in 1972. His best season in County cricket was 1971, with 131 wickets (average 18·89).

Born 29 September 1934, at Georgetown, Guyana. Career aggregate wickets (1953-76): 1024 (average 27·22). Best bowling: 8-37 Warwickshire v Glamorgan, Edgbaston, 1970. 79 Tests – 309 wickets (average 29·09). Best Test bowling: 8-38 v India, Bridgetown, 1961-62.

Grace, Dr. William Gilbert

Despite the fact that so much has been written in praise of W. G. Grace, there may be those who still feel that perhaps time and tradition have exaggerated his greatness, as with other sports stars of long ago. W. G. Grace, however, really was as good as we have been led to believe. Many of the wickets of his day were not of the standard we expect at the present times, and the fact that he scored well over 50000 runs on all types of pitches and captured nearly 3000 wickets speaks for itself. It is also worth remembering that although his career extended over 43 years he never bagged a 'pair'. Add to that his 877 catches and the fact that he captained England in 13 of his 22 Tests, and there can be no doubt that he was one of the game's greatest all-rounders. He also captained Gloucestershire from 1870 to 1899 (sharing the last season with W. Troup). The fourth of five brothers he was only nine when he first played for West Gloucestershire CC. He made 152 in his Test debut against Australia at the Oval in 1880. When he captained England in his final Test against Australia at Trent Bridge in 1899 he was aged 50 years 320 days.

Born 18 July 1848, at Downend, Bristol. Died 23 October 1915, at Mottingham, Kent. Career aggregates (1865-1908): 54896 runs (average 39·55); 2876 wickets (average 17·99). Highest score: 344 for MCC v Kent, Canterbury, 1876. 22 Tests – 1098 runs (average 32·29). Highest Test score: 170 v Australia, Oval, 1886.

The first really great man of cricket, and, 65 years after his death, no doubt still the most easily recognised: Dr W. G. Grace

Hammond, Walter Reginald

A majestic batsman, Wally Hammond enhanced the Gloucestershire side from 1920 to 1951, scoring a record number of runs for them. including 113 centuries. His total of 167 centuries in all first-class matches has been excelled only by Hobbs and Hendren. Hammond, who was born in Kent, scored two separate hundreds in a match a record seven times. His best season was 1933 when he scored 3323 runs (average 67·81). Considering his prowess in Test cricket it is rather surprising that he did not graduate to this class of cricket until 1927-28, when he toured South Africa. His most successful Test series was in Australia the following winter when he created an England Test record by scoring 905 runs (average 113·12). It was on this tour that he scored 251 and 200 in successive Test innings, a performance he excelled in 1932-33 with 227 and 336 not out in successive innings against New Zealand. Apart from his batting he excelled as a slip fielder and his 78 catches in 1928 is another record.

Born 19 June 1903 at Dover, Kent. Died 2 July 1965, at Durban, South Africa. Career aggregate runs (1920-51): 50 493 (average 56·10). Highest score: 336 not out v New Zealand, Auckland, 1932-33. 85 Tests – 7 249 runs (average 58·45).

Harvey, Robert Neil

Only Bradman has scored more Test runs for Australia than Neil Harvey, who appeared for Victoria from 1946 to 1957 and for New South Wales from 1958 to 1963. He was one of the most difficult men to bowl out and excelled on difficult pitches. Small and dapper, he was extremely quick on his feet. Only 19 years of age when he scored 153 for Australia against India at Melbourne in 1948, he also scored 112 against England at Leeds well before his 20th birthday. Thereafter he was a Test regular until 1963 and his total appearances (79) is a record for his country. Often daring in his batting, his total of 834 runs (average 92·66) in the Test series in South Africa in 1952-53 has only been exceeded by Bradman and Hammond. His finest tour in England was that of 1953 when he scored 2040 runs (average 65·80), including an innings of 202 not out against Leicestershire. He scored a total of 21 Test centuries.

Born 8 October 1928, at Melbourne. Career aggregate runs (1946-63): 21 699 (average 50·93). Highest score: 231 not out for New South Wales v S Australia, Sydney, 1962-63. 79 Tests – 6 194 runs (average 48·41). Highest Test score: 205 v South Africa, Melbourne, 1952-53.

Hobbs, Sir John Berry

Considering that Essex rejected his request for a trial it is ironic that Jack Hobbs, the game's most prolific run-getter, made his County Championship debut for Surrey against that county and enjoyed an innings of 155. He was immediately awarded his county cap! When he eventually retired in 1934 Jack Hobbs had scored another 196 centuries in first-class matches and created a record that stands to this day. With a mastery of all the finest attacking strokes and a charm and dignity both on and off the field he was greatly respected by spectators and players alike. His best season was 1925, with 3024 runs (average 70·32), and he scored over 2000 runs in an English season no less than 17 times. In addition to his mastery with the bat he was a brilliant fielder at cover-point. He made his initial Test appearance in Australia in 1907 and his last against the same opposition at The Oval in 1930. During his career he figured in 166 first wicket stands of a hundred or more runs, and his stand with Wilfred Rhodes of 323 at Melbourne in 1911-12 is the highest in England-Australia matches.

Born 16 December 1882 at Cambridge. Died 21 December 1963 at Hove, Sussex. Career aggregate runs (1905-34): 61 237 (average 50·65). Highest score: 316 not out for Surrey v Middlesex, Lord's, 1926. 61 Tests – 5410 runs (average 56·94). Highest Test score: 211 v South Africa, Lord's, 1924.

Hutton, Sir Leonard

Whenever anyone mentions Len Hutton, his innings of 364 for England against Australia at The Oval in 1938 is inevitably recalled. Only Gary Sobers (365 not out) has beaten that score in Test cricket. However, while the Yorkshire batsman's innings was undoubtedly an astonishing achievement (he was at the wicket for 797 minutes – another England record) it was not in itself enough to rank him among the all-time greats. Indeed, the innings has even been criticised because of the length of time it took to make that score on a perfect wicket. No, this beautiful stroke player must rank with the greatest because he carried England's batting almost single handed through a dismal period and because his total of 129 centuries has not been exceeded by more than a half dozen players. In addition his total of Test runs has only been beaten by four other batsmen – three of them with more appearances, and his 1294 runs in June 1949 is a record for a single month. Against the West Indies in 1953-54, he averaged 96·71.

Above *Probably England's best-ever batsman. Jack Hobbs turning a ball high to leg, England v Australia, Trent Bridge, 1930*
Left *Another English opening batsman, another cricketing knight. Len Hutton (left) opening with Cyril Washbrook, with whom he shared a record opening partnership for England of 359 against South Africa at Johannesburg, 1948*

Born 23 June 1916, at Pudsey, Yorkshire. Career aggregate runs (1934-60): 40140 (average 55·51). Highest score: 364 (as above). 79 Tests – 6971 runs (average 56·67).

Harold Larwood bowling in the Headingley Test match of 1930. Larwood was the cricketer most affected by the bodyline controversy, but he was also liked by the Australians and went to live in Australia after his retirement

Larwood, Harold

Harold Larwood's career was largely overshadowed by his part in the unfortunate bodyline controversy of 1932-33, but he was a fast bowler of such accuracy that he earned himself an important place in cricket history quite apart from that affair in Australia. Indeed, there are many who claim that this Nottinghamshire star was the fastest bowler ever and he certainly made it to the top in quick time, for it was after only one season in first-class cricket that he was chosen to play for England against Australia. As a matter of fact he had quite mixed fortunes in Test cricket, culminating in that notorious 1932-33 series (his last) when skipper Douglas Jardine made the most of his speed off the bone-hard pitches. His short-pitched bowling with fielders packed on the leg-side was the most hostile ever seen, and a subject of a protest to the MCC by the Australian Board of Control. It was certainly his most successful Test series with 33 wickets (average 19·51), but there is also no doubt that it took its toll both mentally and physically and he was never the same afterwards.

Born 14 November 1904 at Nuncargate, Notts. Career aggregate wickets (1925-38): 1427 (average 17·51). Best bowling: 9-41 Notts v Kent, Trent Bridge, 1931. 21 Tests – 78 wickets (average 28·41). Best Test bowling: 6-32 v Australia, Brisbane, 1928-29.

Lohmann, George Alfred

Only the serious students of cricket history will appreciate why George Lohmann must be included among the all-time greats, for he is not as well known nowadays as some of his contemporaries, such as Dr. W. G. Grace, George Hirst and Johnny Briggs. Because of ill-health his career was comparatively short, but Dr. W. G. Grace described him as one of the best all-rounders he had ever come across and a 'born' cricketer. In 18 Tests he recorded an average of 10·75 while taking a total of 112 wickets – no other leading Test bowler ever took wickets so cheaply. George Lohmann was a bowler who used his head. He had a natural action and could make the ball break both ways. He also developed as quite a batsman, although he was too often tempted to hit the bowling out of sight. His 8 for 35 in one innings against Australia at Sydney in 1886-87 was one of the finest displays of bowling seen in Tests on that ground. In his most successful series he captured 35 wickets (average 5·80) in South Africa in 1895-96. This remarkable average is not a misprint!

Born 2 June 1865, at Kensington, London. Died 1 December 1901. Career aggregate wickets (1884-97): 1805 wickets (average 13·91). 18 Tests – 112 wickets (average 10·75). Best bowling 9-28 v South Africa, Johannesburg, 1895-96.

Miller, Keith Ross

An outstanding personality, Keith Miller was one of the game's finest all-rounders. Whenever he was on the field the spectators were certain to be entertained, for he was essentially an attacking player who delighted the crowd. He was capable of sustained fast bowling of the most hostile variety and although his batting was not quite the same high standard he was always a powerful driver. Added to this he was a brilliant fielder in the slips. He made his first-class debut with Victoria in 1937 and remained with them until joining the RAAF in 1941. After the war he played for New South Wales from 1946 to 1956. His best Test rubber was that in the West Indies in 1955 when he scored 459 runs (average 73·16) and took 20 wickets (average 32·00). In the final Test of that series he enjoyed an innings of 109 and took 6-107 and 2-58. Between making his Test debut against New Zealand in 1946 and his last appearance for Australia at The Oval

in 1956 he missed only two Tests out of a total of 57.

Born 28 November 1919, in Melbourne, Australia. Career aggregates (1937-1956): 14 183 runs (average 48·90). Highest score: 281 not out for Australians v Leicestershire, Leicester, 1956. 497 wickets (average 22·29). Best bowling: 7-12 for New South Wales v S Australia, Sydney, 1955-56. 55 Tests – 2958 runs (average 36·97); 170 wickets (average 22·97). Highest Test score: 147 v West Indies, Kingston, 1954-55. Best Test bowling: 7-60 v England, Brisbane, 1946-47.

Ranjitsinhji, Maharajah Jam Sahib of Nawanagar

'Ranji' was one of the most accomplished batsmen the game has ever seen. He learnt the rudiments of the game at Rajkumar College, Kathiawar, and perfected his cricket while at Cambridge University. He had an extremely sharp eye and could hook even the fastest bowling. His leg glance was a delight to behold. A Cambridge 'Blue' he joined Sussex in 1895 and played regularly until 1904 when he returned to India. He came back to England to play on a number of occasions and made his final appearance for Sussex in 1920. His best season was 1899 when he scored 3159 runs (average 63·18), but the following season was notable for the fact that he scored five double centuries including 222 and 215 not out in succesive innings for Sussex. His appearance was as immaculate as his batting and with his silk shirt buttoned at the wrists he became one of the most popular cricketers in England. He made 154 not out in his Test debut against Australia at Old Trafford in 1896.

Born 10 September 1872, at Sarodar, Kathiawar, India. Died 2 April 1933, at Dehli, India. Career aggregate runs (1893-1920): 24 692 (average 56·37). Highest score 285 not out for Sussex v Somerset, Taunton, 1901. 15 Tests – 989 runs (average 44·95). Highest Test score: 175 v Australia, Sydney, 1897-98.

Rhodes, Wilfred

Considering that Wilfred Rhodes took more wickets than any other player in the game's history as well as scoring nearly 40000 runs, it is obvious that he must be one of the two or three most talented cricketers ever seen. We should not forget that he also made 708 catches during his career, which extended from 1898 to 1930. A remarkably consistent slow left-arm bowler with a delightful rhythm and a very fine batsman, this Yorkshireman first completed the 'double' in 1903 and repeated this achievement 15 times. In 1909 and again in 1911 he actually exceeded 2000 runs and 100 wickets. In fact he took over 100 wickets in a season 23 times. On a wet wicket he has never been excelled. His Test career extended over 30 years and at the age of 52 years 165 days he was the oldest player ever to appear in a Test (v West Indies, Kingston, 1929-30). When Australia were out for only 36 in less than $1\frac{1}{2}$ hours at Edgbaston in 1902 he took 7-17.

Born 29 October 1877, at Kirkheaton, West Riding of Yorkshire. Died 8 July 1973, in Dorset. Career aggregates (1898-1930): 39802 runs (average 30·83); 4187 wickets (average 16·71) Highest score: 267 not out for Yorkshire v Leicestershire, Leeds, 1921. Best bowling: 9-24, C. I. Thornton's XI v Australians, Scarborough, 1899. 58 Tests – 2325 runs (average 30·19); 127 wickets (average 26·96). Highest Test score: 179 v Australia, Melbourne, 1911-12. Best Test bowling: 8-68 v Australia, Melbourne 1903-04.

Richards, Isaac Vivian Alexander

Since Viv Richards' astonishing display in the Test series in England in 1976 this West Indian from Antigua has been referred to as the Black Bradman. His exuberant batting with Somerset, whom he had joined in 1974, had already made him well-known to the fans in England, but that 1976 rubber (only four years after his first-class debut for the Leeward Islands) marked him out as something extra special in the cricketing world. To begin with he was thought to have been a little too impetuous and likely to throw his wicket away, but he learnt quickly and by 1976 he had overcome this without in any way lessening expectations of thrilling and daring batsmanship when at the wicket. His 829 runs (average 118·42) in the 1976 Test rubber has only been exceeded once each by Bradman, Harvey and Hammond, but Viv Richards amassed his total in only four matches instead of the others' five. In addition to this Viv Richards created a record for a calendar year by scoring 1710 Test runs in 1976.

Born 7 March 1952, St. John's, Antigua. Career aggregate runs (1972-79): 14108 (average 47·37). Highest score: 291 v England, The Oval, 1976. 28 Tests – 2500 runs (average 55·55).

Sobers, Sir Garfield St Aubrun

There is not much doubt that Gary Sobers was the best all-round cricketer the game has ever known. Certainly the statistics would be difficult to argue against, for he appeared in a record number of consecutive Tests (85), scored more Test runs than any other player, and reigns supreme as the only one to take over 200 wickets as well as score over 8000 runs in the highest class of cricket. In addition to this his innings of 365 not out for the West Indies against Pakistan at Kingston in 1957-58 is a

Test record, and he has scored more Test centuries (26) than any other West Indian and captained the West Indies more often than any other player (39 times), leading them to victory against Australia in 1964-65, England in 1966 and India in 1966-67. A left-hander, he made his debut for Barbados in 1953. He also played for Nottinghamshire and South Australia, and captained the Rest of the World to victory in England in 1970. For Notts against Glamorgan at Swansea in 1968 he scored a record 36 (six sixes) off one over, a feat recorded by television and subsequently re-shown for cricket fan's delight.

Born 18 July 1936, at Bridgetown, Barbados. Career aggregates (1953-74): 28315 runs (average 54·87); 1043 wickets (average 27·74). Highest score: 365 not out (as above). Best bowling: 9-49 West Indies v Kent, Canterbury, 1966. 93 Tests – 8032 runs (average 57·78); 235 wickets (average 34·03).

Spofforth, Frederick Robert

Born in Australia of Yorkshire stock, F. R. Spofforth was in his time a unique fast bowler, and although it is nearly 90 years since he played his last game he is still considered to have been one of the fastest of all time. What an impact this player made on his first visit to England in 1878! When the tourists beat a strong MCC side at Lord's by nine wickets in a single day 'The Demon' took 6-4 in only 23 balls including the hat-trick, and followed this with 5-16. Against England at Melbourne in January 1879 his bag was 6-48 and 7-42, including another hat-trick. It has been said that he was often unplayable and the match which has gone down in history as 'Spofforth's match' was the Oval Test of 1882. In England's first innings he took 7-46 but England still seemed certain to win when in their second innings they needed only 34 runs with seven wickets to fall. Spofforth, however, turned in a devastating spell of bowling, taking five wickets for 12 runs, finishing with 7-44. He twice took nine wickets in an innings in England – v Lancs in 1878 and v Oxford University in 1886. He played for Derbyshire 1889-91.

Born 9 September 1853 in Sydney, Australia. Died 4 June 1926 in Surbiton, Surrey. Career aggregate wickets (1874-91): 840 (average 15·05). 18 Tests – 94 wickets (average 18·41). Best bowling: 7-44 v England, Oval, 1882; 7-44 v England, Sydney, 1882-83.

Statham, John Brian

Brian Statham is among the most successful Test fast bowlers in the game's history. He first combined with Frank Tyson and later with Freddie Trueman to provide England with two of the most deadly pairs of fast bowlers this country has ever had. Brian Statham made his debut for Lancashire in 1950 and was in the England side for the first time the following year. His most successful Test rubber statistically was that against South Africa in 1960 when he took 27 wickets (average 18·18) including 11 for 97 at Lord's. He was also particularly devastating in Australia in 1954-55, heading the averages for the tour with 44 wickets (average 14·90). Unlike most bowlers of his type, Statham, who preferred to be called 'George', was most undemonstrative. His best season was 1959 when he took 139 wickets (average 15·01).

Born 17 June 1930, in Manchester, Lancashire. Career aggregate wickets (1950-68): 2260 (average 16·36). Best bowling: 8-34 (15-89 in the match) Lancashire v Warwicks, Coventry, 1957. 70 Tests – 252 wickets (average 24·84). Best Test bowling: 7-39 v S. Africa, Lord's, 1955.

Brian Statham bowling against Australia at Lord's in 1953. Control and accuracy were his weapons

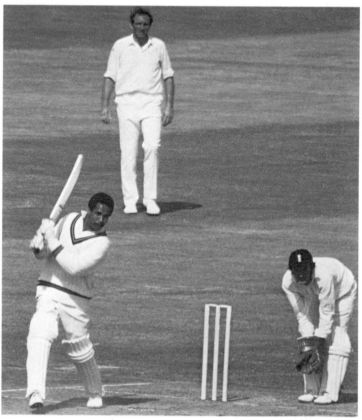

Tate, Maurice William

The powerfully built Maurice Tate was one of the finest seam bowlers of all-time. When he began with Sussex in 1912 he bowled slow-medium off-breaks, but he subsequently abandoned this style and made his name with fast-medium deliveries. England first called on him at the age of 29 and his Test career had a most auspicious beginning. It was the Edgbaston Test against South Africa in 1924 when the visitors were bowled out in three-quarters of an hour for 30. Tate took a wicket with his first ball and completed that innings with 4-12. Arthur Gilligan took the other 6 for 7! Tate's best series was that in Australia in 1924-25 when he captured 38 wickets (average 23·18), a total that has only been beaten by three England bowlers in any series. During his career he probably beat the bat as consistently as any bowler in history. He performed three hat-tricks and his most successful season was 1925 with 228 wickets (average 14·97).

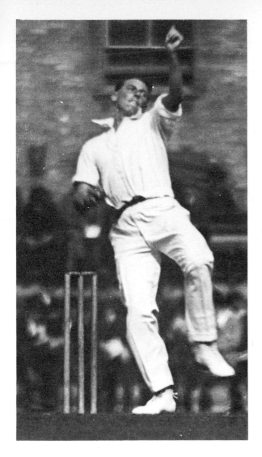

called upon for his first Test series (against India in 1952) he took 29 wickets (average 13·31) in four matches, including one of the most devastating spells of fast bowling ever seen, 8 for 31 in 8·4 overs at Manchester. His most successful Test rubber was against the West Indies in 1963, with 34 wickets (average 17·47). There was another great spell in that series when in the West Indies second innings at Birmingham he took 5 for 0 in 19 balls. In his best season he took 175 wickets (average 13·98) and he performed four hat-tricks during his career.

Born 6 February 1931 at Stainton, Yorkshire. Career aggregate wickets (1949-1968): 2304 (average 18·29). Best bowling: 8-28 Yorkshire v Kent, Dover, 1954. 67 Tests – 307 wickets (average 21·57). Best Test bowling: 8-31 (as above).

*Opposite above Viv Richards running out to drive. He scored a record 1 710 Test runs in 1976
Opposite below Gary Sobers off-driving against England at Lord's, 1973. Alan Knott is the keeper, and Geoff Arnold is in the background
Left Maurice Tate, one of cricket's most popular bowlers, whose deliveries were said to gather speed off the pitch*

Freddie Trueman, whose Yorkshire aggression and irreverent wit, together with his great success, made him one of post-war cricket's outstanding characters

Born 30 May 1895 at Brighton, Sussex. Died 18 May 1956, at Wadhurst, Sussex. Career aggregates (1912-37): 2499 wickets (average 18·07); 21584 runs (average 24·95). Best bowling: 9-71 Sussex v Middlesex, Lord's, 1926. Highest score: 203 for Sussex v Northants, Hove, 1921. 39 Tests – 155 wickets (average 26·13); 1198 runs (average 25·48). Best Test bowling: 6-42 v South Africa, Leeds, 1924. Highest Test score: 100 not out v South Africa, Lord's, 1929.

Trueman, Frederick Sewards

England's most prolific Test wicket-taker, Fred Trueman was also a great character whose outspokenness did not always endear him to the selectors. There was, however, never a more determined fast bowler than this granite-like Yorkshireman, and his good humour both on and off the field endeared him to the fans. He made his debut for Yorkshire in 1949 and when

Trumper, Victor Thomas

Many wonderful stories have been told about Victor Trumper, a delightful batsman who played for New South Wales from 1894 to 1914, when illness cut short his career and soon led to his death. When England visited Australia in 1903-04 it is said that he was so busy in his sports goods shop that he had to make a last-minute dash to reach the ground for the Sydney Test. He grabbed a new bat off the shelf as he set off yet he made 185 not out including a century in 94 minutes. The story does not end there – he sold that bat at a knockdown price because it was second-hand! Considered by many to have been Australia's finest naturally talented batsman, his best series was against South Africa in 1910-11 when he scored 661 runs (average 94·12). On his first visit to England in 1899 he scored 300 not out against Sussex and on his next visit in 1902 hit a century before lunch on the first day of the Old Trafford Test. Figures alone, however, do not do this player justice. All his innings were full of wonderful strokes.

with Worcestershire at Tonbridge. As an all-rounder he is the only man ever to have scored over 2000 runs and captured 100 wickets in as many as four seasons: 1914, 1921, 1922 and 1923. An example of his fast scoring was a triple century in 205 minutes for MCC v Tasmania, at Hobart, in 1912 when he made 305 not out.

Born 2 November 1877 in Sydney, Australia. Died 28 June 1915 in Sydney. Career aggregate runs (1894-1914): 16939 (average 44·57). Highest score: 300 not out (as above). 48 Tests – 3164 runs (average 39·06). Highest Test score: 214 not out v South Africa, Adelaide, 1910-11.

Born 27 May 1887. Died 18 October 1978. Career aggregates (1906-38): 58969 runs (average 40·75); 2068 wickets (average 19·85). Highest score: 305 not out (as above). Best bowling: 8-22 Kent v Gloucestershire, Maidstone, 1921. 64 Tests – 3283 runs (average 36·07). Highest Test score: 154 v South Africa, Old Trafford, 1929. 83 wickets (average 33·91). Best Test bowling: 7-76 v New Zealand, Wellington, 1929-30.

Woolley, Frank Edward

A giant among all-rounders the tall, stylish left-handed Frank Woolley was noted for his coolness, and whether batting or bowling he always made it look easy. In addition to his qualities as a spin bowler and as a fast scoring batsman he was a slip fielder second to none. Some idea of his consistency as a batsman may be had from the fact that he equalled W. G. Grace's record of scoring over 1000 runs in a season as many as 28 times. Even in his last season (1938) when he was 51 years of age he scored 1590 runs, including a century before lunch on the first day of Kent's game

Worrell, Sir Frank Mortimer Maglinne

Frank Worrell, the West Indian all-rounder, is the only man in the game's history to have shared in two stands of over 500 runs – a fourth wicket unbroken partnership of 502 with J. D. C. Goddard for Barbados v Trinidad, Bridgetown, 1943-44, and 574 with C. L. Walcott for the same team against the same opposition at Port of Spain, 1945-46. In the first of those two matches, when Worrell made 308 not out, he was still only 19 years of age. He had a relaxed style but could engender real excitement among the spectators. The fans

will never forget his batting displays during the 1950 Test rubber in England when he headed the West Indies averages with 89·83. At Trent Bridge that summer he scored 239 in a single day's play and went on to make 261. He developed into a fast-medium pace bowler and in the Leeds Test of 1957 took 7-70 in 38·2 overs. Unlike so many of his successors from the West Indies he did not appear in the County Championship and played only for Barbados and Jamaica.

Born 1 August 1924 in Barbados. Died 13 March 1967 in Jamaica. Career aggregates (1942-63): 15025 runs (average 54·24); 349 wickets (average 29·03). Highest score: 308 not out (as above). Best bowling: 7-70 West Indies v England (as above). 51 Tests – 3860 runs (average 49·48); 69 wickets (average 38·73). Highest Test score: 261 v England, Trent Bridge, 1950.

One-day Competitions

Jim Laker

The Gillette Cup

Opposite above
Sussex were the early Gillette Cup kings. Ted Dexter after the defeat of Warwickshire in 1964; S. C. Griffith and G. O. Allen are presenting the medals
Opposite below *Asif Iqbal during his gallant innings against Lancashire in the 1971 Gillette Cup final*

The first Gillette contract agreed in November 1962 was an historic document in cricket history, for it revolutionised our national summer game. At a time when first class cricket was slowly sinking to its knees, with County treasurers worried about being able to foot the bills just to keep the game alive, Gillette cricket injected some new life. It was hard to believe then that a sponsorship originally worth a paltry £6500 would be the forerunner of others, and that a period of 17 years would see sponsorship money increase one hundred fold.

The decision to commercialise the game in this way was by no means unanimous, and the thought of instant one-day cricket of a knock-out nature, surrounded by the razzmatazz of advertisers and banners was something the older die-hard members found impossible to stomach. They were quick to point out that 90 years ago MCC themselves had attempted to promote a knock-out competition which had ended in abysmal failure.

However we live in changing times and today only a small percentage of the public who like watching cricket have the time to sit through a match of three days. The prospect of a game they could see completed in a single day, with a definite result, soon caught their imagination – and that of a new cricket audience. Happily also the Gillette Company have never overplayed their hand and subsequently their long and lasting association with MCC has been built on mutual respect. To put the record straight that original figure of £6500 has steadily increased over the years and has now risen to exactly £100000. Of even greater interest, the gold medals presented to the Man of the Match at every Gillette game were originally purchased for £14. Their present value is £202.50.

If the financial structure has changed a good deal over 17 years then the rules of the competition have scarcely altered, proof surely of the immense appeal of the Gillette Cup. At first the games were scheduled to be played over 65 overs per side, with each bowler allowed a maximum of 15, but several dusk finishes, which gave a great advantage to the side batting first, persuaded the organisers that 60 overs was a more realistic figure, with each bowler restricted to 12 overs. That a bowler is restricted to a certain number of overs has been a bone of contention though at the time it was felt that if this was not the case the cricket would develop into a wearisome exhibition of fast medium defensive bowling to the total exclusion of the spinners. In fact many counties, though not always the successful ones, immediately discarded the slower bowlers and played instead a couple of accurate medium pacers who could also make runs. Thankfully in recent years it has been proved time and time again that the accurate spinner will invariably finish with better figures than an inferior medium or fast bowler. There still remains the thought, however, that limited over cricket penalises the bowler on top of his form, as he cannot bowl more than the stipulated number of overs whereas the batsman has no such limitations, being allowed to bat through the full 60 overs. One side issue of this is that the majority of match awards go to the batsmen, for whom there is a reasonable chance of making 50 or upwards, whilst it would take a really fine performance for a bowler to take five wickets or more in the space of just 12 overs.

The Gillette Cup has remained a firm favourite with the vast majority of cricket supporters and has converted to the one-day game many who previously could see no further than County or Test cricket.

They now appreciate that 60-over cricket, if not always the more abbreviated versions, seldom degenerates into a slogging contest from the word go. A batsman can build an innings and a bowler can bowl, at least in the early stages, to a reasonably attacking field. A Gillette final which includes a fine variety of cricket spread over 7½ hours and normally producing around 450 runs is remarkably good value for anyone's money and will continue to pack Lord's for many years to come.

Two of the more memorable of those Lord's finals took place in 1968 and 1971. Sussex, winners in the first two years, returned to Lord's to play Warwickshire in 1968 and to all intents and purposes were quietly coasting to a third victory. Their score of 214 for 7 included 57 and 41 respectively from the old firm of Parks and Greig, and after an early burst from Jim Stewart the Warwickshire wickets tumbled quickly. Amiss alone held fast and with a 9, 10 and 'Jack' of no great repute it seemed that Warwickshire's only hope was that Alan Smith might drop anchor and leave the scoring to Amiss. Indeed the reverse was the case, as the Warwickshire wicket keeper cut loose with a range of strokes previously confined to the Oxford nets, and amid great excitement was undefeated with 39 as he made the winning hit.

Three years later those old antagonists and previous winners Lancashire and Kent were locked in a mighty struggle. Clive Lloyd had led the way with a fine 66 in Lancashire's score of 224 for 7. It all seemed too much for Kent until Asif Iqbal decided to play one of the most memorable of all Gillette final innings. He had reached 89 in such sparkling form that it seemed the 24 runs now required were possible in only 2 or 3 overs. Once again he danced down the pitch, cracked the ball hard and high to the right of Jack Bond. The diminutive Lancashire skipper leapt feet in the air and grabbed a great one-handed catch when all seemed lost.

Gillette Cup history is full of great matches and high drama and one could not believe that the epic encounter between Lancashire and Gloucestershire in the 1971 semi final, when David Hughes cut loose to crack the winning runs as dusk settled over the ground, could ever be bettered. However eight years later at the same stage of the competition 574 runs were scored in a single day with the sides finishing with

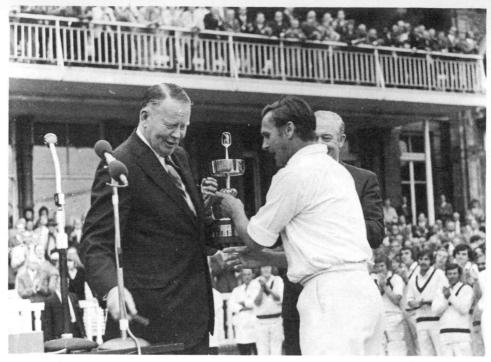

Jack Bond of Lancashire receives the 1971 Gillette Cup from F. R. Brown. Bond's tremendous catch to dismiss Asif was the turning point of the match

287 each. The venue was a Taunton ground packed to suffocation and the match featured two of the newer rivals in first-class cricket, Somerset and Essex. The brilliance of Viv Richards, with a score of 116, was instrumental in the home side's final total of 287 for 6. Essex, with plenty of strength and depth, are a good batting side and the wicket was perfect, but 288 looks a long way away with Garner and Botham firing on all cylinders. Gooch and Fletcher in particular gave Essex more than an outside chance, Hardie and Pont with some spectacular hitting kept up the good work. However they were both run out, as indeed was Phillip, and the 60th and final over saw Smith and Lever, the last pair, together. Hardened supporters could barely watch as 3 runs were needed for victory from the very last ball. Lever faced and managed to turn a single into a comfortable two. Having lost more wickets than Somerset they had to go for a third, but despite some measure of panic in the field there was no real hope, Smith was run out and Somerset were through. This was Gillette Cup cricket at its very best: hard, competitive, with no favours asked or given, yet played in a spirit which was a credit to both sides.

It would be foolish to think that Gillette cricket will always produce thrills such as this but the percentage of good cricket in a 60-over match remains high, with the result that its future is secure for some time to come.

John Player League

The Cavaliers, sponsored by Rothmans, first saw the possibilities of Sunday afternoon cricket geared to television, on which the entire game could be watched from start to finish. It was an instant success, with enormous attendances watching many of the household names who formed the basis of Cavalier cricket, and who travelled from far and wide to play against various counties. Some quite substantial sums were handed over to county beneficiaries, many charities and indeed to MCC themselves. From the Cavaliers' viewpoint it was all too good and too successful to last. As the authorities at Lord's began to realise the potential they could not accept that it was right and proper for an outside organisation to be creaming off large sums. After all MCC were the ruling body who for years had ploughed vast amounts into the development of the game at grass roots. Here was an opportunity to help to balance the budget, not only at Lord's but around the struggling counties. From their position of power they quickly placed a ban on contracted players participating in Cavalier cricket, and by arrangement with the counties saw that the principal grounds were no longer available to them.

This virtually meant the end of the Rothman Cavaliers, and even more an end to Rothmans' major involvement in cricket sponsorship. Worse news for them was the fact that their rivals in the tobacco industry, John Player Ltd, would be the sponsors in a new Sunday League to start in 1969 involving all the first class counties. Each county would receive £3000 with an extra £1000 to the winners of the League and £500 to the runners-up.

Our cricketers were scarcely over enthusiastic for many reasons, not least being the £50 to be shared amongst the winning teams each Sunday. The sponsors themselves made their first mistake when giving this new league the title of The Players League which left many people believing it was the cricketers themselves who had organised it. The company very rapidly put matters right and in 1970 it became known as the John Player League. On reflection, it was a fairly disastrous start all round. Rain fell steadily throughout May, only five County Championship matches produced a result, the touring West Indians sat cold, wet, and miserable in pavilions up and down the country and Warwickshire for one saw exactly one quarter of their new Sunday fixtures completely washed out.

The players remained very sceptical, for in addition to the scant financial rewards the new league meant virtually the end of the Sunday benefit games which accounted for a large percentage of the benefit 'take.' Often long journeys were necessary to complete these fixtures, and with bowlers' run-ups reduced to 15 yards many of the pace bowlers found problems in adjusting, especially in the middle of a three-day county game. The games could begin only at 2pm, and geared as they were to full television coverage they had to be restricted to 40 overs each side.

The cynics, of course, did not consider such encounters to be real cricket and many players did not take too kindly to the rough and tumble tactics required. In fairness the majority were willing to give this new format an extended trial, and surely but slowly they began not only to come to terms with it but finally quite to enjoy it. As the years have gone by they have changed their techniques and discovered that a limited amount of 40-over cricket can in fact improve in several ways many aspects of their game. Most certainly

A straight drive from Gordon Greenidge for Hampshire against Middlesex in the John Player League, 1978. Greenidge is a matchwinner in John Player cricket

it has brought about a vast improvement in fielding standards and field placings. Batsmen have improved their range of strokes and bowlers have bowled more accurately.

Sponsorship money has become greater, and with large gate receipts continually building up the John Player League has become established as a vibrant, necessary and enjoyable fixture in the cricket calendar. Its popularity throughout the country can be judged on television audience figures, which have more than quadrupled since those early and doubtful days.

The theory that 40-over cricket is something of a lottery has been laid to rest when one considers that only four teams share nine of the 11 titles to date. Kent (3), Lancashire (2), Leicestershire (2) and Hampshire (2) have led the way, with Essex seldom out of the hunt. All these teams have depth in batting, plenty of reserve bowling strength and an acute awareness of the timing of a 40-over match.

Individually the game has been dominated by overseas players. Greenidge and Richards of Hampshire have both exceeded 150 in a single innings and Glenn Turner of Worcestershire is ahead in aggregate runs. Keith Boyce with a best-ever bowling performance of 8 for 26 reached the double of 1000 runs and 100 wickets in only 51 matches. In nine of the first 11 seasons the fastest televised 50 has gone to overseas players, with Majid Khan reaching that score in just 22 balls.

The last word on the ultimate success of the John Player League came from the previously unheralded county of Somerset. After over 100 years of striving for any sort of honour they finally captured the Gillette Cup and took the John Player title on successive days. Their eight home Sunday fixtures brought in record receipts of almost £36000, final proof of the success of a competition which has increased in popularity and prestige with each succeeding year.

Benson and Hedges Cup

It was in 1971 that Gallaher Ltd, the parent company of Benson and Hedges, looked very closely at their sporting commitments and decided to extend them further. Fortunately for cricket, Peter West at that time had taken over as adviser in his Public Relations capacity, and he managed to persuade them that there was good value and high mileage in cricket sponsorship. At Lord's it was agreed that the game could just about stand a third one-day competition without overloading the programme and after a number of lengthy meetings a format of value to all parties concerned was agreed. To avoid a clash with the Gillette Cup the new Benson and Hedges Cup would be played during the first 12 weeks of the season, culminating

Opposite left Barry Richards hitting through the covers. He and his opening partner Greenidge have each topped 150 in John Player matches
Opposite right The best-ever John Player bowling performance was achieved by all-rounder Keith Boyce
Below The enthusiasm for one-day cricket is shown by the crowd participation in the Benson and Hedges final of 1978 between Kent and Derbyshire

The 1979 Benson and Hedges final: Gooch drives Intikhab square during his century for Essex against Surrey

minor counties side, and this should certainly create new interest.

Looking to avoid any sort of confusion with the Gillette Cup, the Benson and Hedges is played over 55 overs per side, with each bowler allowed a maximum of 11 overs, and whereas Gillette nominate for each and every game a Man of the Match, Benson and Hedges talk in terms of the Gold Award which falls nicely in line with their general advertising theme. The original sponsorship fee of £80000 per year has now shot up to £160000 and as the best part of £33000 is distributed as prize money to teams and individual players it comes as no surprise that the Benson and Hedges is greeted with real enthusiasm, particularly by the players.

From time to time serious doubts have been expressed concerning the period covered by Benson and Hedges cricket, i.e. from April through to June. It certainly cuts into the time available for first-class cricket leading up to the first Test match, and consequently hinders the selectors and gives fewer opportunities for likely contenders for Test match honours to prove themselves. However, it would be unjust to the sponsors if changes devaluing the competition were introduced. Their financial contribution is generous when one considers that only four matches are televised compared to the 19 Sundays allocated on BBC2 to the John Player League. After all, without television coverage all forms of sports sponsorship would fall alarmingly.

A great deal of thought has been given to the promotional value by Benson and Hedges and if anyone ever doubts the value of Public Relations they should look closely at the expert and efficient manner in which it is handled in this particular event. When all is said and done the success of the competition lives or dies on the interest it creates and the crowds that attend. Crowds will only roll up if the cricket warrants it. There can be no doubt that Benson and Hedges cricket has finally caught the imagination of players and public alike, never more so than in the 1979 final. A packed Lord's ground warmed to the sight of Keith Fletcher triumphantly holding the trophy sky high. Essex will forever be grateful that the sponsors provided the opportunity for them to collect their first major prize in their long and distinguished history.

in a Lord's final before the Gillette Cup was seriously under way.

Searching for something that would add variety to the season, and wishing to avoid a sudden death knock-out competition which would not be of much financial aid to more than half the counties, it was resolved to adopt a similar system to that used in the last few soccer World Cup finals. The country was split into four zones with five teams in each playing each other. The two top teams in each zone would go forward to the quarter-finals and the Cup concluded on a knock-out basis. With 20 teams taking part and only 17 first class counties the first problem was to find three teams to fill those vacancies. This has been a major problem for eight years now and various permutations have been tried. The minor counties have supplied a couple of specially selected sides and have failed to register a victory, though since Oxford and Cambridge Universities joined forces they have fared considerably better. The latest and as yet untried idea is for a representative side from Scotland to join a combined

Prudential World Cup

The most ambitious of all sponsored one-day cricket competitions has been Prudential's support of the World Cup. Admittedly it has to date taken place on only two occasions, in 1975 and again in 1979, yet it has been such an unqualified success that there can be little doubt that it is certain to be a permanent fixture every four years. Both times it was played the venue has been England, and although there have been proposals that the tournament in future should be hosted in other countries, there are several factors which suggest that the World Cup will continue to be held here. Most important is that in midsummer 120 overs can be completed very comfortably in good light in England in a single day. There would be great difficulties in trying to get in this amount of cricket in Australia, West Indies, India or Pakistan.

In 1975 the Prudential Assurance Company put forward the sum of £100000 to start the ball rolling and the Prudential World Cup was born. With South Africa unacceptable, the six leading cricket playing countries formed the basis of the competition, but as the new format re-quired eight countries to play in two groups of four on a league system, invitations were extended to Sri Lanka and East Africa.

The draw for groups A and B were made at Lord's and resulted as follows:

Group A	Group B
England	Australia
India	Pakistan
New Zealand	West Indies
East Africa	Sri Lanka

Thus England were fortunate to draw the weaker section, and it looked as if a real old tussle would take place in group B. As anticipated the games in group A turned out to be very predictable. East Africa were completely out of their depth and New Zealand were the only country to offer any serious challenge to England. They were beaten by 80 runs at Trent Bridge, one of six Test grounds used throughout the competition. The one really competitive fixture was between India and New Zealand to decide which of them would go through with England to the semi-final. New Zealand finally triumphed with just seven balls to spare, thanks to a superb undefeated century by Glenn Turner.

The crowd invade the pitch after West Indies second Prudential World Cup win in 1979

A packed ground for the first Prudential World Cup final at Lord's in 1975: West Indies playing Australia

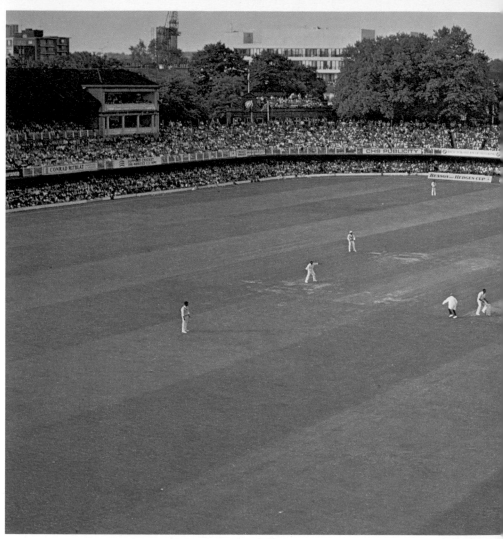

Some of the squad of players from the 21 countries to take part in the Prudential World Cup of 1979: from left, Sri Lanka, Pakistan, West Indies, England, Australia, New Zealand, India, Canada

Another six? Clive Lloyd, hero of West Indies 1975 win, hooking high and handsome

Group B provided much more entertainment when the favourites, West Indies, only managed to overcome Pakistan by the skin of their teeth. Australia too were really shaken by the outsiders Sri Lanka. In a most courageous performance at the Oval the Sri Lankans, chasing an Australian score of 328 for 5, reached a magnificent total of 276 for 4 before time ran out for them. Lillee, Thomson and Mallett between them had figures of 2 for 136!

In the semi-finals England were to meet Australia at Headingley and West Indies were to clash with New Zealand at the Oval. In Yorkshire England were destroyed by Gary Gilmour on a helpful pitch with the astonishing figures of 6 for 14. He followed this with the top score of 28 not out to bring victory for his side by 4 wickets in a contest which altogether lasted only 65 overs. West Indies quietly and efficiently moved through to meet Australia in the final with a comfortable 5-wicket margin against the Kiwis.

The final proved to be a memorable occasion in every way. Record receipts of £66950, two fine sides locked in combat from 11 am to 8.45 pm, 565 runs scored, and all on a perfect summer's day. Clive Lloyd's 102 and his partnership of 149 in 36 overs with Kanhai saw West Indies to a score of 291 for 8. Thanks to Turner and Ian Chappell Australia put up a great fight but some suicidal running between wickets combined with brilliant fielding by Kallicharan and Richards saw four men run out, and at 233 for 9 the cause, it seemed, was lost. Suddenly both Lillee and Thomson, in a last ditch attempt, began to throw the bat. Now the West Indies looked rattled as the last pair added 41, but with only 17 wanted from the last eight

Gary Gilmour scotched England's hopes in 1975 with 6-14 in the Prudential semi-final. Here Dennis Amiss is lbw, Barry Wood the non-striker

Group 1	P	W	L	NR	Pts
Bermuda	4	3	0	1	14
East Africa	4	2	1	1	10
Papua New Guinea	4	1	1	2	8
Singapore	4	1	2	1	6
Argentina	4	0	3	1	2
Group 2					
Denmark	4	4	0	0	16
Canada	4	3	1	0	12
Bangladesh	4	2	2	0	8
Fiji	4	0	3	1	2
Malaysia	4	0	3	1	2
Group 3					
Sri Lanka	4	2	1	1	10
USA	4	2	1	1	10
Holland	4	1	2	1	6
Israel	4	1	3	0	4
*Wales	4	2	1	1	—

balls Thomson became the fifth player to be run out, and West Indies became the first holders of the Prudential World Cup.

In 1979 a much more ambitious scheme was evolved. No fewer than 15 member countries of the ICC were invited to play for a separate ICC Trophy, with the finalists going to the World Cup proper. These were split into three groups of five, and 32 matches were played on Club grounds in the Midlands. The semi finalists were the Group winners plus the runners up with the best points tally. The final outcome was as shown in the following tables.

In Group 3 Sri Lanka went forward on a faster scoring rate than USA and had a comfortable win over Denmark whilst Canada beat Bermuda by four wickets. The ICC trophy was won by Sri Lanka in a final dominated by the batsmen of both sides, with no fewer than 588 runs scored in a day on the true Worcester pitch.

So it was that Canada and, once again, Sri Lanka joined the big league with the former grouped with Australia, Pakistan and England in Group B and the latter

Majid Khan and Zaheer Abbas nearly toppled the West Indies in the 1979 Prudential final. Here Majid edges past Greenidge

*Wales played as substitutes, but were not eligible for competition, not being full Associate Members of ICC

with West Indies, New Zealand and India in Group A. Sri Lanka, who had threatened a giant killing act four years previously, overcame their great rivals India and even took two points from the mighty West Indians in a rain ruined fixture. Yet predictably it was West Indies and New Zealand who went on from Group A to the semi finals. The disappointment in Group B was the poor showing of Australia, whose solitary success was against the Canadians, leaving England and Pakistan in the top two positions.

At the Oval West Indies played Pakistan and England met New Zealand at Old Trafford. If the eventual outcome of these games proved the experts to be correct, there were times in both matches when the result may well have been reversed. Although the West Indies totalled 293, Pakistan at one stage were 176 for 1 with Majid and Zaheer in full cry. Another half hour together and the game could have been settled in their favour, but in the end the Antiguan combination of Roberts and Richards proved too much. England, too, had a few anxieties before scrambling home by nine runs, the narrowest margin in any Prudential Cup match.

The final, played under ideal conditions and resulting in another West Indian victory by the large difference of 92 runs, may on the face of it appear to have been too one-sided to be of great interest. This

was never the case, for at 99 for 4 the West Indies were in real trouble. They managed to escape due to an amazing selectorial blunder on the part of Brearley and Co. With Willis unfit to play, the selectors went into the match, on a perfect pitch, with only four front line bowlers, and opted to use three batsmen, Gooch, Boycott and Larkins to bowl the additional 12 overs. More so they were used in turn at the most critical time of the West Indian innings against Richards and King. The pair of them scored 138 not out and 86 respectively and the combined bowling figures of Gooch, Boycott and Larkins read 12 – 0 – 86 – 0!

Thus West Indies' total of 286 was just about 30 or 40 runs too many. At one stage England were 183 for 3 with 13 overs left, though there had not been sufficient urgency from either Brearley or Boycott, the chief scorers. As a result too much pressure was placed on the remaining batsmen, and in a quite sensational spell of pace bowling from Garner and Croft England lost their last eight wickets for only 11 runs in just 26 balls. In fact justice was done, and for the second time in four years the best side had won the Prudential Cup.

Although the unkind weather in 1979 compared with the wonderful summer of 1975 was a slight disappointment it was certainly not reflected in gate receipts. The total take of £188598 in 1975 was almost doubled four years later when the figure had leapt to an incredible £359717. Even now the odds must be still in favour of a West Indian hat trick in 1983.

Collis King square cuts in the Prudential final of 1979. His innings of 86 turned the match. Bob Taylor is the wicketkeeper

Joel Garner was the final destroyer of England, mopping up most of the last eight wickets in two overs

Overleaf An early triumph for England (left) in the Prudential Cup Final of 1979, as Mike Hendrick bowls Alvin Kallicharan round his legs, but ultimate victory for West Indies (right) as Clive Lloyd holds the trophy on the balcony at Lord's

The Winners of the One-day Competitions

Year	Gillette Cup	John Player League	Benson and Hedges Cup	Prudential World Cup
1963	Sussex			
1964	Sussex			
1965	Yorkshire			
1966	Warwickshire			
1967	Kent			
1968	Warwickshire			
1969	Yorkshire	Lancashire		
1970	Lancashire	Lancashire		
1971	Lancashire	Worcestershire		
1972	Lancashire	Kent	Leicestershire	
1973	Gloucestershire	Kent	Kent	
1974	Kent	Leicestershire	Surrey	
1975	Lancashire	Hampshire	Leicestershire	West Indies
1976	Northamptonshire	Kent	Kent	
1977	Middlesex	Leicestershire	Gloucestershire	
1978	Sussex	Hampshire	Kent	
1979	Somerset	Somerset	Essex	West Indies

The Game Today

Alan Lee

It is only a few years ago that the image of a batsman wearing a protective helmet and pastel-coloured clothing, and playing under blazing floodlights, would not have been deemed futuristic, but plain absurd. The perpetrator of such a cricketing forecast would have been told that there was no room for his sort of poppycock in this game, old chap...

Today, if not universally approved, such innovations are accepted as being among the inevitable inheritance as the game moves inexorably into the commercial age. There is, it seems, no turning back now. Cricket, however much of a wrench it may seem to those who cling steadfastly to traditional values, will never be quite the same again.

While most of the developments within the game would have surely occurred naturally at some time, there can be no doubt that cricket's progress into an entirely new era was dramatically accelerated by the World Series Cricket project, supported and presided over by the man who will forever stir the most fervent reactions among cricket people, Kerry Packer.

If Packer had not seen the potential, of a business nature, in the dissatisfaction growing rampant among the leading players of the mid-1970s and acted upon it in such devastating fashion, 1980 may well have dawned with the game not appreciably different.

Instead, although the ruling bodies have survived unaltered, the business machine has begun operating within cricket. The top players are now earning amounts more in keeping with their equals in other sports; almost every competition, down to the minor club leagues and tournaments, has the name of a sponsor attached; advertisers and commercial backers are being sought with ever-increasing zest by county clubs who would previously have been alarmed by the very idea. For the players, as well as the administrators, cricket has entered the age of the brief-case.

So, some would argue, Mr Packer and World Series Cricket have a great deal to answer for. Depending on one's stance in the matter, that may be so – fewer players would agree than might be expected – but it always has to be remembered that the seeds, for the birth of WSC's staggering operations, were planted by a number of cricketers fed up with getting meagre

Kerry Packer (left) *and Tony Greig outside the Law Courts in 1977. They brought about the biggest changes in cricket for years*

rewards for the talent of their output. WSC's aims, apart from making money for its backers, were to improve the lot of those players . . . and to present the game as the public wanted to see it.

Up to a point, they succeeded. New television concepts gave the presentation of cricket previously unseen dimensions. Other promotional ideas in the cities and on the grounds thrust the game at the people. Some of the schemes were no better than cheap gimmicks; others were sheer inspiration by men whose job, after all, had always been to market a certain product.

Whatever the ethics and morals of the Packer affair, it has had a profound effect on the sport it held to ransom. Above all else, it has given the players a new and elevated status, or at least made them believe they can achieve it, and exerted far heavier financial responsibilities on the people who run cricket at the top.

In August of 1979, England's national team put in a request for a wage rise. They were not satisfied with the offer made by the Test and County Cricket Board for their projected winter tour of Australia, and asked for a considerable increase. It was a unique situation. A national team of cricketers were acting like any other body of workers and, if their attitude was not exactly a threat to strike, it certainly amounted to something like a shop-floor revolution . . . even before the 16 names for the tour had been chosen!

This was not the first example of leading cricketers joining together in actions more readily associated with a trade union. In March of 1978, the West Indies were playing a home series against Australia. World Series players were included by the West Indies, but not by Australia, and when, for the Third Test, three Packer players were dropped by the West Indian selectors, the rest refused to play.

In Australia, a Players' Association was set up by the World Series players, led by Ian Chappell and Ian Redpath, and quickly made itself heard and felt. Players there were professional, for the first time, and as WSC wound up in the wake of Packer's truce with cricket officialdom, men like the Chappell brothers, who had previously announced their retirement from Test cricket, indicated that they were ready to return in a full-time capacity.

Back in England, the Test squad took on a promotional and marketing company as their commercial agents. Nobody in the game's hierarchy actually approved, but there was nothing whatever they could do about it. They could not deny that, as professionals at the peak of their career, Test cricketers had been woefully paid for many years. Now they were doing something about it.

Many of the England side had personal agents in addition, arranging their appearances, negotiating deals with clothing manufacturers, kit-makers, publishers and newspapers, and generally fielding the business phone calls which the players themselves did not want to take.

The pioneer of this burgeoning commercial awareness had perhaps been Tony Greig, still seen by a proportion of the cricket public as a Judas Iscariot for his recruiting activities within the Packer network at the very time that the England side was developing improved form and spirit under his captaincy. Greig had an

Ian Chappell hits a six for Australia against West Indies in a one-day match at Adelaide in 1975. Later he became a leading light in a Players' Association

agent before most other players had thought it proper, let alone profitable, and made such use of the opportunities that his business acumen caught, and ultimately overtook, his enthusiasm for playing the game. Greig was motivated by a burning ambition which made him animated at each new scheme. He never really understood why people despised him for actions which, to his mind, were designed only to improve himself and, subsequently, the lot of the players, and at first the animosity hurt. But he found new outlets in Australia, where Packer himself set up an insurance company and made Greig managing director. The last I heard, he was smoking a fat cigar, and enjoying the idyllic life in a house with pool, barbecue area and ballroom, all set off with a staggering view of Sydney's most exclusive bay.

Greig made people think. Even those whose dislike of what he had done remained rampant for months, years even, were forced to admit he had been influential in giving the game new directions.

The media, of course, doted on him for his controversial views and actions, and cricket subsequently achieved a greater and more regular airing on television and in newspapers. In turn, businesses became alert to the possibilities of linking their name with the game ... and cricket found some sponsors.

Naturally, that is a very basic explanation of a phenomenon in which Greig played only a minor role, if an important one. The need of sponsors in the game had long been apparent, even to the most radical Long Room speechmaker. Without them, full-time cricket would die.

It began gently, with Gillette in 1963, gathered pace with the John Player and Benson and Hedges competitions, became international with the Prudential and finally brought forward backers for the two most important competitions – the County Championship and the Test Series.

Schweppes took on the Championship, the flagging three-day game, and the counties breathed a sigh of relief. Threatened by doubling expenses and diminishing attendances, a number of them were teetering around a financial crisis, and this new injection of cash and goodwill gave them breathing space.

Test match sponsorship was unwittingly spawned by Packer himself. As the game reeled somewhat drunkenly, tried to reassure itself that it would all blow over and finally conceded that it might not, David Evans, a London businessman, made an ambitious announcement that he would attempt to find the money to buy out the English Packer recruits and then pay each England player £1 000 per Test. The effect was quite startling. Within a matter of days, Mr Evans had been contacted by the Cornhill Insurance group. Within weeks, agreement was reached with the Test and County Cricket Board and they became the official sponsors of English Test cricket for a sum of around one million over five years.

It could be, indeed has been, argued that cricket sold its premier showpiece too cheaply. Nevertheless, by 1977, every major English competition was sponsored and each new one appeared to come with its backer intact.

If some of the credit for the progress belongs to the players and their improved projection, the majority certainly rests with the astute individuals within the Test and County Cricket Board. And, although a greater share of responsibility and authority was probably due to the players, none in their senses would wish to challenge the game's administrative ladder.

At the head of that ladder, and in theoretical control over the broad spectrum of world cricket, stands the ICC – the International Cricket Conference. This comprises representatives from each member country and wields the greatest power over any major policy changes affecting the running of Test cricket.

Only the six Test-playing countries are full members: England, Australia, West Indies, New Zealand, India and Pakistan. Other cricket-playing nations possess associate membership and some, like Sri Lanka, have justifiable hopes of gaining promotion to the elite.

Since the incursions of Mr Packer, the ICC have endured some traumatic times, in and out of the law courts. There were occasions when its unity appeared dangerously flimsy, particularly over the issue of including WSC players in Test teams, and for one torrid period the entire Test cricket system, already temporarily weakened, looked set for a further, irreparable split.

Not blind to such appalling prospects, the ICC worked stealthily and skilfully to bring about an acceptable peace treaty to the greatest upheaval in sporting history. Their structure had wobbled, but it was sound enough to survive the storm and continue, hopefully to more tranquil years.

Below the ICC on cricket's tree of power each country has its own Board of Control, responsible for domestic first-class cricket and for the affairs of their own national side when playing at home.

In England, that authority is in the hands of the Test and County Cricket Board, who administer the 17 first-class counties – all of whom have their representative on the Board – and the home Test matches played by the England team. They also conduct negotiations with prospective and current sponsors, television companies and advertisers, revise the laws of the game whenever necessary – especially relevant these days with the changing demands of the various limited-over competitions – and have a sub-committee responsible for all disciplinary matters.

The rest of English cricket, notably clubs and schoolboys, is controlled by the National Cricket Association which, like the TCCB, is based at the games's headquarters, Lord's.

There is still a place in cricket for the most famous authority of them all, the Marylebone Cricket Club, and the privilege of wearing their red and yellow 'eggs and bacon' tie has never diminished. Their power has, however, and they no longer have any great influence over the game as a whole. Even the national touring team, which travelled abroad under the MCC banner for a century, is now more realistically identified as England.

Tours have increased in regularity recently, and there is considerably more Test cricket played now than even a decade ago. During the English winter of 1979-80, for instance, India participated in 13 Test matches...and that after completing a World Cup competiton and a four-Test series in England during the summer of 1979. There are many who believe that the Test programme is being overcrowded to a stifling extent, and more than one distinguished Test cricketer has expressed fears that his career at the top will be cut dramatically short by the heavy demands on stamina and mental fitness.

Floodlit cricket was another diversion introduced by WSC

If it is true that there is more cricket played than ever before, then it also follows that the pressures on players are greater – because of the prominence they have achieved in the leisure and entertainment worlds. The eye of the media never leaves them now, nor do the demands of the business world and, indeed, the ordinary cricket fan.

Floodlit cricket, still in its infancy, could exert still greater pressures. The matches begin in early afternoon and continue until after ten at night, and the players who took part in the WSC promotion discovered that they were required to alter their personal time-clocks quite appreciably. There is no gain, for instance, in rising at the normal hour of eight o'clock – normal that is, for a normal cricket match! – and breakfasting with five or six hours to spare before the day's active work begins. Nor, for most players, is there any percentage in rushing back from the evening session and falling into bed. A wind-down period is

Mike Brearley was one of the first cricketers to wear head protection. On the left he is batting in his original skull cap with protective flaps, on the right with his 1979 helmet and visor. Ironically, in the picture he has just been hit and cut on the forehead by a ball from Ghavri in the MCC v India match at Lord's

Andy Roberts of West Indies, rated just about the best fast bowler of the late 1970s

Brearley believed that the top-class pace bowlers, while not necessarily quicker through the air than their predecessors, were more methodically intimidating in their use of the short-pitched delivery. It follows that Brearley was among the first to advocate and then wear a protective helmet.

The design of Brearley's pioneer helmet was basic – a skull cap made of toughened plastic, with thickly-padded flaps protecting the vulnerable temple regions. He wore it, with some success, for more than a year before it was rendered obsolete by more sophisticated models. First, the crash-hat of motor-cyclist style used and marketed by England's Dennis Amiss, and then the design which was intrinsically more acceptable, made to resemble an ordinary cricket cap, with peak and visor attachments for those who wanted them.

In 1979, they were adopted generally for the first time. Almost every English county placed an order for helmets, and very few leading batsmen had not worn one at some time. Even Geoff Boycott, who had previously declared that he was a little long in the tooth for such changes, used a helmet in the World Cup Final of 1979, to face the mighty, four-pronged speed attack of the West Indies.

It was the plethora of pace bowlers, allied to their conveyor-belt supply of natural, stroke-playing batsmen, which had established the West Indies as the most formidable team of the 1970s. Under the captaincy of the vastly-respected Guyanan-cum-Lancastrian, Clive Lloyd, they had won the first World Cup, in 1975, survived a stunningly heavy defeat in Australia the following winter, then developed their side in terms of both talent and temperament. They were outstanding in one-day cricket, where their impetuous, explosive belligerence was less likely to come to grief, and they dominated the limited-overs tournaments of World Series Cricket, to which almost all of their best players had committed themselves, before returning to England to defend and retain the World Cup in 1979.

Andy Roberts was their enduring spearhead, a bowler rated the best in his business by almost all who had faced this lean, slightly stooping and chiefly silent man from the miniature island of Antigua. He spent five seasons with Hampshire, but was only truly effective for two; always, his

necessary, which means that it is well past midnight before the majority retire, well after nine when they surface again. Many still look sceptically upon night cricket as foolish gimmickry, but there is no doubt it has attracted a new and wide audience to the grounds and the television screens of Australia; whether it would work in the less clement climates of other cricket nations is doubtful.

The modern players' theory, supported by these and other facts, is that the actual cricket is also sterner than ever before. For a reason, one may need to look no farther than the high rewards offered for success nowadays, but there is also the probability that tactics are more aggressive and more physically threatening.

This was the view of Mike Brearley, England's captain from 1977 to 1980 and without doubt one of the game's finest minds, let alone most successful skippers.

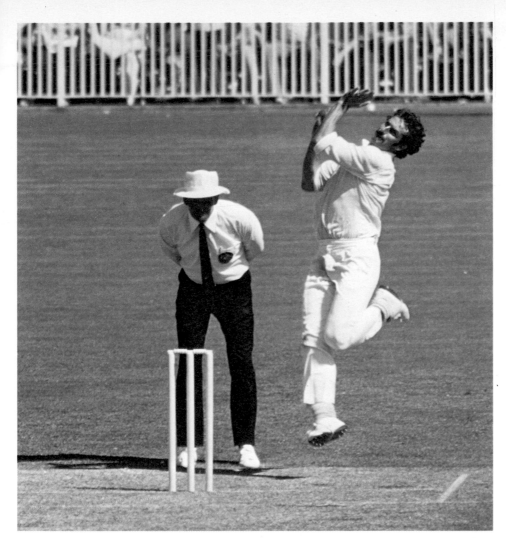

greatest efforts were reserved for the international stage, where his classically rhythmical action was a sheer delight to all those not on the receiving end. He reached 100 Test wickets in a shorter calendar time than any previous bowler – a record later improved by England's Ian Botham – and was still averaging five wickets per match when his Test career resumed in the winter of 1979-80.

Most countries would have been pleased to have one bowler of similar pace and hostility to support Roberts. The West Indies had four... Michael Holding, Wayne Daniel, Colin Croft and Joel Garner, each of individual style but all of a speed to instil apprehension, if not outright fear.

Holding is an athlete, a tall, slender man who runs in with poetical bounds and bowls probably as quickly as anyone of his frame could possibly achieve. He de-

vastated England during the 1976 season, capping his feats with 13 wickets on a typically flat Oval pitch, but has since been plagued by injury.

Daniel's build is entirely different. A broad, muscular man, he negotiated early problems of run-up when his Test career began at the age of 19, and has bowled with quite awesome pace for his country and for Middlesex.

Croft and Garner are the giants, totalling well over 13 feet tall, and both use their height to its best advantage. Garner, in particular, emerged with such impact during the late 1970s that most batsmen agreed he was the most difficult of bowlers to play, simply through the abnormal bounce he was able to achieve.

The West Indies have always had class fast bowlers; equally, they have constantly been blessed with gifted, spectacular batsmen. Over the past three decades, the

A Jeff Thomson thunderbolt on its way. Thomson and Lillee are Australia's best opening pair since Lindwall and Miller

Bob Willis following through against New Zealand at Lord's 1978. Willis has been England's leading fast bowler through the late 1970s

names roll deliciously off the tongue of anyone who watches cricket – Worrell, Weekes and Walcott, Sobers, Hunte and Kanhai, and now the butchering powers of Gordon Greenidge and the almost uncanny attacking talent of Vivian Richards.

Greenidge is the archetypal Barbadian; round-faced, well-built and with a bat wielded like a sledge-hammer. Richards is the languid type, who looks as if the last thing on his mind is the savage destruction of anything one might care to bowl. Like Roberts, he is an Antiguan, and it is a chilling fact for all who oppose the West Indies that these two cricket masters should be contemporaries on such a tiny island.

During the early and mid-1970s, the West Indies fought a battle for supremacy with the Australians, led first by Ian Chappell and then by brother Greg. With Dennis Lillee and Jeff Thomson reaching peaks of pace bowling to rival any comparable pairing of the past, the scene was set for the contest to continue throughout the decade...until Packer scooped every Australian star into his pool.

No country can expect to replace an entire team, a winning team at that, and remain successful. The Australians inevitably struggled for two years, and their problems ran deeper than poor results. Bitterness between players was bound to

Above *South African Mike Procter, perhaps the best all-rounder of the 1970s, whose best efforts were for Gloucestershire*

Above right *Graham Dilley of Kent, given his big chance by being included in the England party to tour Australia, 1979-80*

Opposite *David Gower, seen scoring off his legs for England against Pakistan at The Oval in 1978, is the most elegant batsman to have emerged in the 1970s*

scar the post-Packer years, particularly when the stars, their WSC activities complete, expected to be taken back into the Test fold immediately.

England had suffered less severely at the hands of Packer. Perhaps only Derek Underwood of the defectors was sorely missed, although none can deny the abilities of his Kent and WSC colleagues, Bob Woolmer and Alan Knott.

In their absence, Mike Brearley led a re-shaped team through a period of startling success. True, they were able to avoid the West Indies, and played Pakistan and Australia when those sides were badly understrength. But there was a new mettle about this England side, inspired quietly by the academic Brearley and the converted character of Bob Willis, once a likely lad but thriving on new responsibilities with a serious and determined outlook.

Ian Botham, the muscular Somerset all-rounder, emerged to break records with his remarkably early progress in the Test arena; David Gower, the young blond left-hander, arrived with an elegance not seen in an England batsman for years past;

Geoff Boycott ground out runs with the inevitability of a computer. It was a well-rounded England side, capable and competent if not among the great teams.

Elsewhere, Pakistan stuttered from promise to promise, never quite fulfilling the vast potential that they appeared to have; India continued to rely extensively on the genius of their mini-masters, Gavaskar and Viswanath; New Zealand produced several splendid batsmen but only one world-class bowler in the lively Richard Hadlee.

South Africa continued to suffer their exile, while their cricketing sons, from the experienced Barry Richards and Mike Procter to the precocious Allan Lamb, Kepler Wessels and Garth Le Roux, made their runs and took their wickets as reluctant mercenaries, deprived, by a political crisis of which they wanted no part, of making up what would surely have been one of the greatest teams ever.

Cricket had never been richer, yet never more vulnerable to the vulgar forms of gimmickry which could alienate so many. The 1970s had been torrid and traumatic. The 1980s needed delicate handling.